BCBA Exam Prep A Study Guide to Practice Test Questions With Answers and Master the Board Certified Behavior Analyst Examination

Table of Contents

Introduction

Welcome to the world of Board Certified Behavior Analysts (BCBAs), where you work tirelessly to improve the lives of individuals with behavioral challenges. This noble profession requires dedication, expertise, and a deep understanding of applied behavior analysis (ABA). The journey towards becoming a BCBA is rigorous and demanding, culminating in the BCBA certification exam – a pivotal moment in your career.

For aspiring and current BCBAs alike, this book is designed to be your trusted companion on the path to success. Our mission is simple: to help you navigate the intricate landscape of the BCBA exam with confidence and competence. Whether you're a student preparing for the exam for the first time, a professional seeking re-certification, or a practicing BCBA looking to reinforce your knowledge, this book provides a comprehensive resource filled with practice test questions and detailed answers to ensure you are well-prepared.

The BCBA certification is more than just a piece of paper – it's a symbol of your commitment to improving the lives of individuals with behavioral challenges. It signifies that you have met the highest standards of competence and ethics in the field of applied behavior analysis. Achieving BCBA certification opens doors to various career opportunities in the field, including roles in education, clinical settings, and research.

However, earning the BCBA credential is no walk in the park. It requires you to have a profound understanding of the principles and concepts of applied behavior analysis, as well as the ability to apply this knowledge effectively in real-world situations. The BCBA exam is a crucial step in this process, evaluating your readiness to take on this role.

The BCBA exam is known for its difficulty, and for good reason. It is a comprehensive assessment that covers a wide range of topics related to applied behavior analysis. From the foundational principles of behavior to the application of ABA techniques in various settings, the exam is a true test of your knowledge, problem-solving skills, and ability to make ethical decisions. It consists of multiple-choice questions, requiring you to choose the best answer from a set of alternatives.

What makes the BCBA exam particularly challenging is its depth. You will need to demonstrate a profound understanding of ABA concepts, and this includes a deep familiarity with relevant terminology, research, and practical applications. You must be able to analyze complex scenarios and select the most appropriate interventions. The exam's rigidity necessitates extensive preparation.

The road to BCBA certification begins with comprehensive preparation. In your journey to becoming a BCBA, you've likely encountered various resources – textbooks, coursework, seminars, and supervision. While these resources are invaluable, what often distinguishes successful candidates from those who struggle is the quality and quantity of practice questions.

This book is designed to be your ultimate resource for mastering the BCBA exam. It is not intended to replace your textbooks or coursework but to complement them. In these pages, you will find a vast collection of practice test questions, carefully curated to represent the wide array of topics and concepts you'll encounter on the BCBA exam. Each question is accompanied by a detailed answer and explanation to ensure that you not only memorize the material but deeply understand it.

The questions in this book are not mere rote memorization exercises; they are designed to challenge your critical thinking, problem-solving abilities, and your capacity to apply ABA principles in real-world scenarios. By immersing yourself in this extensive question bank, you will gain the knowledge, skills, and confidence needed to succeed on the BCBA exam.

This book is structured to provide a comprehensive and focused approach to BCBA exam preparation. We have organized it into sections that correspond to the key content areas covered by the exam, including:

- Foundational Knowledge: These questions will test your understanding of basic ABA principles, terminology, and the history of behavior analysis.

- Measurement: Explore questions related to data collection, graphing, and statistical analysis – all critical aspects of ABA practice.

- Experimental Design: Test your knowledge of research methods and experimental design, a vital skill for analyzing and evaluating behavioral interventions.

- Behavior Change Considerations: Questions in this section examine ethical considerations, behavioral assessments, and intervention strategies.

- Fundamental Elements of Behavior Change: Gain a deep understanding of reinforcement, punishment, stimulus control, and other key concepts.

- Specific Behavior Change Procedures: These questions focus on the application of ABA techniques in various settings, including schools, clinics, and homes.

- Client-Centered Responsibilities: Explore the ethical and professional responsibilities that come with being a BCBA.

Each section is preceded by a brief overview of the topic and followed by an extensive set of practice questions and detailed answers. As you progress through the book, you'll have the opportunity to test your knowledge, identify areas that require further study, and gain valuable insights into the BCBA exam's structure and content.

Throughout this book, we emphasize the importance of ethical behavior analysis practice. As BCBAs, you are not only responsible for improving behavior but also for adhering to a strong code of ethics. These principles are woven into the fabric of the BCBA certification and should guide your professional behavior throughout your career. We encourage you to consider the ethical implications of each question you encounter.

To get the most out of this book, we recommend the following study approach:

Begin by familiarizing yourself with the content areas and topics covered by the BCBA exam. Use this book as a supplementary resource alongside your primary textbooks and coursework.

As you work through each section, start with the practice questions. Answer them to the best of your ability, but don't worry if you get some wrong. The goal is to learn, and making mistakes is an essential part of the learning process.

After attempting the questions, review the answers and explanations provided. Pay close attention to any concepts or topics that you found challenging.

Keep a notebook or digital document to jot down key concepts, terminology, or strategies you want to revisit or further explore.

Continuously track your progress and set goals for improvement. Revisit the sections that you find most challenging and reattempt the questions until you feel confident in your understanding.

Becoming a BCBA is a noble and rewarding pursuit. This certification represents your dedication to enhancing the lives of individuals with behavioral challenges. It is also a testament to your commitment to ethical practice in the field of applied behavior analysis.

Throughout this journey, the BCBA exam stands as a significant milestone, requiring a thorough understanding of ABA principles and their practical application. This book is here to guide you through this challenging process, offering a wealth of practice test questions and detailed answers to help you achieve success.

Embrace this resource as your study companion, and embark on your path to BCBA certification with confidence and competence. By mastering the BCBA exam, you are one step closer to making a profound impact on the lives of those in need. Good luck in your journey, and may this book serve as your trusty guide on the path to excellence in applied behavior analysis.

Chapter 1: Foundations of Applied Behavior Analysis – Introduction to ABA Principles

Applied Behavior Analysis (ABA) is a well-established and highly effective approach for understanding and modifying human behavior. Grounded in the principles of learning and behavior, ABA has found widespread application in diverse fields, from psychology and education to clinical and organizational behavior management. In this chapter, we will delve into the foundational principles of ABA, providing a comprehensive introduction to its key concepts, theories, and methodologies.

The Roots of Applied Behavior Analysis

The origins of ABA can be traced back to the early 20th century when psychologists and behaviorists began to explore the relationship between environmental factors and human behavior. The behaviorist movement, led by notable figures such as John B. Watson and B.F. Skinner, emphasized the idea that behavior is shaped by the environment and that it can be understood and controlled through the principles of learning.

John B. Watson: The Father of Behaviorism

John B. Watson, a pioneering American psychologist, is often referred to as the father of behaviorism. In 1913, he published the groundbreaking paper "Psychology as the Behaviorist Views It," in which he advocated for the objective study of behavior and the rejection of introspection. Watson believed that all behavior is learned through conditioning, and he paved the way for the development of behaviorism as a dominant school of thought.

B.F. Skinner: The Father of Operant Conditioning

B.F. Skinner, another influential figure in the development of ABA, built upon Watson's ideas. He is renowned for his work on operant conditioning, a process by which behavior is modified through consequences. Skinner's work with reinforcement and punishment laid the foundation for many ABA principles. His research introduced concepts like positive and negative reinforcement, shaping, and extinction, which are central to ABA practice.

Key Concepts of Applied Behavior Analysis

To understand ABA fully, it's essential to grasp the core concepts that underpin its practice. ABA principles are built upon a set of foundational ideas that guide the analysis and modification of behavior. Let's explore some of these key concepts:

Behavior

In ABA, behavior is the focal point of study. Behavior is defined as any observable and measurable action, including verbal and non-verbal actions. This emphasis on objectivity and measurability sets ABA apart from other psychological approaches, allowing for precise data collection and analysis.

Environment

The environment encompasses all external factors that influence behavior. These factors can include physical surroundings, social interactions, and sensory stimuli. A central tenet of ABA is that behavior is a product of interactions with the environment, and it can be understood and influenced through the manipulation of these environmental variables.

Stimulus

A stimulus is any event or condition that can influence behavior. Stimuli can be classified as antecedents (events that precede behavior) and consequences (events that follow behavior). ABA practitioners examine how different stimuli elicit and maintain behavior, allowing them to develop effective interventions.

Contingency

A contingency refers to the relationship between a specific behavior and its consequences. In ABA, behaviors are often examined in terms of their contingencies – what happens immediately before and after a behavior. Understanding these contingencies is crucial for designing interventions that promote desired behaviors.

Reinforcement

Reinforcement is a fundamental concept in ABA. It refers to the process of strengthening a behavior by following it with a consequence that increases the likelihood of that behavior recurring. Reinforcement can be positive (adding a stimulus to increase behavior) or negative (removing a stimulus to increase behavior).

Positive reinforcement involves adding something desirable (e.g., praise or a reward) to increase the frequency of a behavior. Negative reinforcement involves removing something aversive (e.g., turning off an annoying noise) to increase behavior. Both forms of reinforcement play a vital role in shaping behavior.

Punishment

Punishment is the process of weakening a behavior by following it with a consequence that decreases the likelihood of that behavior recurring. Like reinforcement, punishment can also be positive (adding something aversive) or negative (removing something desirable). However, it is important to use punishment judiciously and ethically, as it can have unintended side effects.

Extinction

Extinction is the process of reducing a behavior by discontinuing the reinforcement that previously maintained it. When a previously reinforced behavior is no longer followed by reinforcement, it may decrease in frequency. Extinction is a crucial tool in behavior modification, especially when trying to eliminate unwanted behaviors.

Stimulus Control

Stimulus control is the phenomenon in which a behavior occurs more frequently in the presence of specific stimuli. ABA practitioners use stimulus control to teach individuals to respond to particular cues or prompts, leading to more adaptive and context-appropriate behaviors.

Generalization

Generalization is the process of applying learned behaviors in new or different situations. ABA aims to teach behaviors that are not limited to specific settings, ensuring that individuals can adapt their skills across various contexts and environments.

Data Collection

One of the hallmarks of ABA is the systematic collection of data. ABA practitioners use various methods to measure and record behavior, enabling them to analyze patterns, track progress, and make data-driven decisions about interventions.

The ABCs of Behavior Analysis

To effectively apply ABA principles, professionals use the ABC model – Antecedent, Behavior, Consequence. This model provides a structured approach to understanding and modifying behavior. Let's break down the ABCs:

Antecedent

The antecedent, often referred to as the "A," is the event or circumstance that occurs before a behavior. It sets the stage for the behavior to occur. Antecedents can be environmental cues, verbal instructions, or internal thoughts and emotions.

Behavior

The "B" represents the observable behavior itself. This is the action or response that occurs in reaction to the antecedent. Behaviors can be as diverse as a child raising their hand in class, a person saying "hello" when greeted, or someone clenching their fists in frustration.

Consequence

The "C" represents the outcome or event that follows the behavior. Consequences can either reinforce or punish the behavior.

Data Collection and Measurement

Precise measurement and data collection are central to ABA practice. Behavior analysts use various methods to gather data and track behavior over time. This data allows for objective assessment of progress and informs the selection of interventions. Common methods for data collection include:

Direct Observation: Behavior analysts often observe behavior in its natural setting to collect baseline data. Observations are typically conducted systematically and include detailed descriptions of the behavior.

Interval Recording: This method involves dividing the observation period into intervals and recording whether the behavior occurred during each interval. It provides a snapshot of when the behavior is happening.

Duration Recording: Duration recording measures the total time a behavior occurs. This is particularly useful for behaviors that have a significant impact over time, such as self-injury.

Frequency Count: Behavior analysts record how many times a behavior occurs within a specified period. This is effective for tracking behaviors that have distinct, countable occurrences.

Latency Recording: Latency recording measures the time between the presentation of an antecedent and the initiation of the behavior. It helps identify any delays in response.

Accurate data collection is essential for understanding the behavior, assessing the effectiveness of interventions, and making data-driven decisions in ABA.

The Role of Reinforcement

In ABA, reinforcement is a powerful concept. Reinforcement is the process of increasing the likelihood that a behavior will occur again in the future by following that behavior with a consequence that is pleasurable or desirable to the individual. Reinforcers can take various forms, such as tangible items (e.g., toys or treats), attention, praise, and access to preferred activities.

Reinforcement is essential in behavior change. ABA practitioners use reinforcement strategies to strengthen desired behaviors and teach new skills. Positive reinforcement involves adding something rewarding after the behavior, while negative reinforcement involves removing something aversive or undesirable.

For example, if a child completes their homework (the behavior) and receives praise from their teacher (the positive reinforcement), they are more likely to complete their homework in the future. Similarly, if a person wears a seatbelt (the behavior) to avoid an annoying seatbelt alarm (the negative reinforcement), they are more likely to continue wearing their seatbelt.

The Ethical Foundation of ABA

The practice of ABA is rooted in a strong ethical framework. The Behavior Analyst Certification Board (BACB) has established a comprehensive Code of Ethics that guides the professional behavior of individuals in the field. These ethical guidelines emphasize principles such as beneficence (acting in the best interest of clients), non-maleficence (avoiding harm), and respect for autonomy.

ABA practitioners are ethically bound to provide effective and evidence-based interventions, respect the rights and dignity of their clients, and maintain professional competence. Ethical considerations are woven into every aspect of ABA practice, ensuring that individuals receiving ABA services are treated with the highest standards of care and respect.

The foundations of Applied Behavior Analysis are deeply rooted in a rich history of scientific exploration and understanding of human behavior. ABA principles, with their emphasis on the ABCs, the function of behavior, data collection, reinforcement, and ethics, have become essential tools for improving the lives of individuals with autism, developmental disorders, and those facing various behavioral challenges.

Chapter 2: Concepts and Principles

This chapter will explore concepts such as reinforcement, punishment, behavior functions, and assessment methods, providing a comprehensive understanding of how ABA principles are applied in practice.

The ABCs Revisited

To grasp the essence of ABA, it's crucial to revisit the ABCs - Antecedents, Behavior, and Consequences. These three components are the building blocks of ABA analysis and intervention.

Antecedents: As mentioned in Chapter 1, antecedents are the events or circumstances that precede a behavior. They set the stage for behavior to occur, and understanding them is essential for identifying behavior triggers.

Behavior: Behavior is the observable and measurable action or response of an individual. Precise and objective descriptions of behavior are crucial in ABA.

Consequences: Consequences are the outcomes or events that follow a behavior. They can be reinforcing (increasing the likelihood of behavior repetition) or punishing (decreasing the likelihood of behavior recurrence). In ABA, the role of consequences is central to modifying behavior.

Reinforcement

Reinforcement is a fundamental concept in ABA and is essential for behavior change. It is the process of increasing the likelihood that a behavior will recur in the future by following it with a consequence that is pleasurable or desirable to the individual. Reinforcers can take various forms, such as tangible items, attention, praise, or access to preferred activities.

There are two main types of reinforcement:

Positive Reinforcement: Positive reinforcement involves adding something desirable or rewarding after a behavior occurs. For example, a teacher may provide verbal praise to a student for completing their homework, making it more likely that the student will complete their homework in the future.

Negative Reinforcement: Negative reinforcement involves removing something aversive or undesirable after a behavior. For instance, wearing a seatbelt in a car to silence an annoying seatbelt alarm is an example of negative reinforcement. The removal of the aversive sound makes it more likely that the individual will continue to wear their seatbelt.

Reinforcement is a powerful tool in shaping behavior. ABA practitioners use reinforcement strategies to increase desirable behaviors and teach new skills effectively.

Punishment

Punishment is another essential concept in ABA. It is the process of reducing the likelihood of a behavior recurring in the future by following it with a consequence that is aversive or undesirable to the individual. Like reinforcement, punishment can also take two forms:

Positive Punishment: Positive punishment involves adding something aversive or undesirable after a behavior occurs. For example, if a child talks back to a teacher and is given detention as a consequence, it's an example of positive punishment. The addition of detention makes it less likely that the child will talk back to the teacher again.

Negative Punishment: Negative punishment involves the removal of something desirable or rewarding after a behavior. For instance, if a teenager is caught breaking curfew and loses their privileges to go out with friends, it's an example of negative punishment. The removal of the privilege decreases the likelihood of the teenager breaking curfew in the future.

Punishment, while sometimes necessary, should be used cautiously in behavior modification. ABA practitioners prioritize using reinforcement strategies whenever possible and consider punishment as a last resort.

Functions of Behavior Revisited

In Chapter 1, we introduced the idea that all behavior serves a function. This concept is central to ABA, as it guides the understanding and modification of behavior. Behavior can be categorized into four main functions:

Escape/Avoidance: Individuals may engage in a behavior to escape or avoid a situation or demand they find aversive. For example, a student might refuse to do their homework to avoid the aversive task.

Attention-Seeking: Some behaviors are maintained because they result in attention from others. A child may engage in disruptive behavior to gain the attention of their parents or teachers.

Access to Tangible Items: Individuals may engage in behaviors to access desired items or activities. For example, a child might cry to get a favorite toy.

Automatic Reinforcement: Certain behaviors may be intrinsically reinforcing, providing sensory pleasure or satisfaction. An individual might engage in self-stimulatory behavior like hand-flapping because it produces sensory enjoyment.

Identifying the function of behavior is crucial for developing effective interventions. By understanding why a behavior occurs, ABA practitioners can tailor strategies to address the underlying need or motivation.

Assessment Methods

To conduct effective behavior analysis and intervention, ABA practitioners use a variety of assessment methods. These assessments help in understanding the behavior, identifying its function, and creating targeted intervention plans. Common assessment methods in ABA include:

Functional Behavior Assessment (FBA): FBA is a systematic approach to identifying the function of behavior. It involves collecting data on antecedents, behavior, and consequences, and analyzing this information to determine the underlying cause or function of the behavior.

Preference Assessments: These assessments help identify preferred reinforcers. ABA practitioners use preference assessments to determine the most effective reinforcers for a particular individual, which is crucial for behavior modification.

Direct Observation: Direct observation is an ongoing process in ABA, involving systematic and objective data collection through the observation of behavior. It helps in tracking progress and assessing the effectiveness of interventions.

Structured Interviews: ABA practitioners often conduct interviews with caregivers or individuals themselves to gather information about behavior, antecedents, and consequences. This information is valuable in understanding the context and triggers of behavior.

Functional Analysis: A functional analysis is a controlled experiment designed to test and verify the hypothesized function of a behavior. It involves manipulating antecedents and consequences to determine their impact on the behavior.

Reinforcement and punishment, the functions of behavior, and assessment methods are fundamental components of ABA practice. These concepts are the building blocks for understanding and modifying behavior effectively. In the following chapters, we will explore how ABA principles are applied in various settings, including education, therapy, and daily life, to improve the lives of individuals with behavioral challenges.

These concepts lay the foundation for understanding behavior and the methods used in ABA. Let's dive into each of these key concepts and provide examples to illustrate their significance.

2: Stimulus and Stimulus Class

Stimulus: In ABA, a stimulus is any event or situation that can influence or evoke a response. Stimuli can be visual, auditory, tactile, olfactory, or even internal, like thoughts and emotions. They play a crucial role in behavior analysis as they are often used to prompt or shape behaviors.

Example: Imagine a teacher presenting a math problem on the chalkboard. The math problem displayed on the chalkboard is a stimulus that prompts the student to solve it.

Stimulus Class: A stimulus class refers to a group of stimuli that share common features or characteristics, and a response to one stimulus in the class may generalize to other stimuli within the same class.

Example: If a child learns to identify the letter 'A' in different fonts, the ability to recognize 'A' will generalize to various fonts of the letter, creating a stimulus class.

3: Respondent and Operant Conditioning

Respondent Conditioning: This type of conditioning involves the learning of associations between stimuli and involuntary reflexive responses. It is typically associated with classical or Pavlovian conditioning, where a neutral stimulus (conditioned stimulus) becomes associated with an unconditioned stimulus, leading to a conditioned response.

Example: When a dog associates the sound of a bell (neutral stimulus) with the arrival of food (unconditioned stimulus) and salivates in response to the bell alone, this is an example of respondent conditioning.

Operant Conditioning: Operant conditioning focuses on the relationship between behavior and its consequences. It explores how behaviors are strengthened or weakened based on the outcomes they produce, such as reinforcement or punishment.

Example: If a student is praised (positive reinforcement) for completing their homework and, as a result, continues to complete assignments, this is an example of operant conditioning.

4: Positive and Negative Reinforcement Contingencies

Positive Reinforcement: Positive reinforcement involves presenting a desirable stimulus or consequence immediately after a behavior occurs, which increases the likelihood of that behavior happening again.

Example: If a child is given a piece of candy (desirable stimulus) after cleaning their room (behavior), and they clean their room more frequently in the future, this is an example of positive reinforcement.

Negative Reinforcement: Negative reinforcement involves the removal or avoidance of an aversive stimulus following a behavior, which also increases the likelihood of that behavior occurring again.

Example: When a driver fastens their seatbelt (behavior) to turn off an annoying seatbelt alarm (removal of an aversive stimulus), they are negatively reinforced to wear a seatbelt in the future.

5: Schedules of Reinforcement

Schedules of reinforcement determine when and how often reinforcement is delivered following a behavior. There are two main types: continuous reinforcement (reinforcement is given every time a behavior occurs) and intermittent reinforcement (reinforcement is given sporadically).

Example: In intermittent reinforcement, there are various schedules, such as fixed-ratio (reinforcement after a fixed number of responses) and variable-interval (reinforcement after varying time intervals). An example of this is a slot machine, which provides intermittent reinforcement based on a variable ratio schedule.

6: Positive and Negative Punishment Contingencies

Positive Punishment: Positive punishment involves the presentation of an aversive stimulus following a behavior, which decreases the likelihood of that behavior occurring again.

Example: If a child is scolded (aversive stimulus) for taking a cookie without permission (behavior), and they are less likely to take cookies without permission in the future, this is an example of positive punishment.

Negative Punishment: Negative punishment entails the removal of a desirable stimulus following a behavior, which also decreases the likelihood of that behavior happening again.

Example: When a teenager loses their driving privileges (removal of a desirable stimulus) due to irresponsible behavior, they are negatively punished, and the irresponsible behavior may decrease.

7: Automatic and Socially Mediated Contingencies

Automatic Contingency: In an automatic contingency, the consequences of behavior are a direct result of the behavior itself, without the involvement of another person.

Example: If a child repeatedly touches a hot stove and gets burned, the pain experienced is an automatic consequence of their behavior.

Socially Mediated Contingency: Socially mediated contingencies involve the influence of others' behavior as part of the consequence.

Example: When a child's tantrum (behavior) results in their parent providing a desired toy (consequence), this is a socially mediated contingency.

8: Unconditioned, Conditioned, and Generalized Reinforcers and Punishers

Unconditioned Reinforcer/Punisher: Unconditioned reinforcers or punishers are inherently reinforcing or punishing and do not require prior learning. Examples include food as a reinforcer and pain as a punisher.

Conditioned Reinforcer/Punisher: Conditioned reinforcers or punishers acquire their value through association with other reinforcers or punishers. Money, for example, is a conditioned reinforcer because it has value due to its association with obtaining goods and services.

Generalized Reinforcer/Punisher: Generalized reinforcers or punishers are stimuli that can be exchanged for a wide range of other reinforcers or punishers. Money, again, is an example because it can be used to obtain various goods and services, making it a generalized reinforcer.

9: Operant Extinction

Operant extinction involves the withholding of reinforcement previously provided for a behavior, resulting in a decrease in the frequency of that behavior.

Example: If a child has been receiving attention for tantrums and suddenly, the parent ignores the tantrums, the tantrum behavior may decrease due to operant extinction.

10: Stimulus Control

Stimulus control refers to the influence of antecedent stimuli on behavior. It means that certain behaviors are more likely to occur in the presence of specific stimuli.

Example: A teacher giving a math problem (antecedent stimulus) may lead a student to engage in math problem-solving behavior but not during a history class.

11: Discrimination, Generalization, and Maintenance

Discrimination: Discrimination is the ability to respond differently to different stimuli or situations. It involves recognizing and responding to specific cues.

Example: A dog may sit when the owner says "sit" but not when a friend says the same word, demonstrating discrimination.

Generalization: Generalization occurs when a behavior that was learned in one situation carries over to other similar situations or settings.

Example: A child who learns to say "please" when asking for a toy at home might also use the same polite language when asking at school.

Maintenance: Maintenance refers to the persistence of a behavior over time, even after the initial intervention or training has ended.

Example: A child continues to use good manners (saying "please" and "thank you") months after they were initially taught these behaviors.

12: Motivating Operations

Motivating operations are environmental factors that temporarily change the effectiveness of a reinforcer or punisher. They can make a consequence more or less reinforcing.

Example: If a child is hungry (increasing the value of food as a reinforcer), they may be more motivated to complete their meal to access the food.

13: Rule-Governed and Contingency-Shaped Behavior

Rule-Governed Behavior: Rule-governed behavior is behavior controlled by verbal or written instructions, such as following rules, laws, or guidelines without direct experience.

Example: A driver follows the speed limit because they read and understand the rule even without getting a speeding ticket.

Contingency-Shaped Behavior: Contingency-shaped behavior is behavior that has been directly shaped by its consequences.

Example: A child learns to ride a bike through trial and error, with their behavior shaped by the consequences of staying balanced.

14: The Verbal Operants

The verbal operants are categories of language functions identified by B.F. Skinner. They include mand, tact, echoic, intraverbal, textual, and transcription. Each serves a different communicative purpose.

Example: A "mand" is a verbal operant used to request something, like saying "water" when thirsty. A "tact" is used to label or describe something, such as calling a tree a "tree."

15: Derived Stimulus Relations

Derived stimulus relations refer to the ability to respond to stimuli based on learned relationships, even if these relationships were not explicitly trained.

Example: If a person learns the relationship between A and B and between B and C, they may also derive the relationship between A and C without direct training.

Understanding these concepts and principles is essential for effective practice in ABA. They form the basis for analyzing and modifying behavior in diverse settings, from clinical therapy for individuals with autism to classroom management, and even organizational behavior management in the workplace. In the subsequent chapters, we will continue to explore the practical application of these concepts and principles in various contexts and settings.

Chapter 3: Foundations, Concepts, and Principles

In this chapter, we will continue to explore the foundational elements, concepts, and principles of Applied Behavior Analysis (ABA). We'll cover a wide range of topics, from the philosophical underpinnings of ABA to the essential aspects of measurement, data display, and interpretation. This chapter is divided into several sections to facilitate your understanding of these key principles.

I. SECTION 1: Philosophical Underpinnings

1. Identify the Goals of Behavior Analysis as a Science

The fundamental goals of behavior analysis as a science are to understand, predict, and influence behavior. This involves systematically studying the principles and laws that govern behavior, discovering ways to predict how behavior will change under various conditions, and developing effective interventions to improve behavior.

2. Explain the Philosophical Assumptions Underlying the Science of Behavior Analysis

The science of behavior analysis is rooted in several philosophical assumptions, including determinism (the belief that all behavior has identifiable and lawful causes), empiricism (relying on objective observation and measurement), and parsimony (preferring simple explanations when multiple interpretations are possible).

3. Describe and Explain Behavior from the Perspective of Radical Behaviorism

Radical behaviorism, associated with B.F. Skinner, emphasizes the importance of the environment in shaping behavior. It considers both observable behavior and the events that control behavior, placing a strong focus on the analysis of operant behavior and the impact of consequences.

4. Distinguish Among Behaviorism, the Experimental Analysis of Behavior, Applied Behavior Analysis, and Professional Practice Guided by the Science of Behavior Analysis

Behaviorism is a broad field that studies behavior in various contexts. The Experimental Analysis of Behavior focuses on studying behavior in controlled settings, often using non-human subjects. Applied Behavior Analysis (ABA) applies the principles of behavior analysis to practical, real-world situations, while professional practice guided by the science of behavior analysis refers to implementing ABA principles in professional settings, like clinical therapy or education.

5. Describe and Define the Dimensions of Applied Behavior Analysis (Baer, Wolf, & Risley, 1968)

In 1968, Baer, Wolf, and Risley defined the seven dimensions of ABA: Applied, Behavioral, Analytical, Technological, Conceptually Systematic, Effective, and Generality. These dimensions serve as a guide for evaluating and conducting ABA interventions, ensuring that they are relevant, scientifically sound, and socially significant.

II. Concepts and Principles

1. Define and Provide Examples of Behavior, Response, and Response Class

Behavior: Behavior refers to any observable and measurable action, reaction, or activity of an individual.

Response: A response is a specific instance of behavior, often occurring as a reaction to an antecedent stimulus.

Response Class: A response class is a group of behaviors that share similar functions or serve the same purpose. For example, various vocalizations can belong to the same response class if they all function to request attention.

2. Define and Provide Examples of Stimulus and Stimulus Class

Stimulus: A stimulus is any event or condition that can influence or evoke a response. An example is a teacher's instruction (stimulus) prompting a student to raise their hand (response).

Stimulus Class: A stimulus class consists of stimuli that share similar characteristics and can evoke similar responses. For instance, all red objects in a room could be considered a stimulus class.

3. Define and Provide Examples of Respondent and Operant Conditioning

Respondent Conditioning: Respondent conditioning involves the learning of associations between stimuli and involuntary reflexive responses. For example, associating the sound of a bell with salivation (Pavlov's experiment).

Operant Conditioning: Operant conditioning explores the relationship between behavior and consequences, strengthening or weakening behaviors based on their outcomes. An example is a child completing chores to earn an allowance (positive reinforcement).

4. Define and Provide Examples of Positive and Negative Reinforcement Contingencies

Positive Reinforcement: Positive reinforcement involves providing a desirable stimulus following a behavior to increase the likelihood of that behavior happening again. Giving praise for completing homework is an example.

Negative Reinforcement: Negative reinforcement entails removing an aversive stimulus following a behavior, also to increase the likelihood of that behavior recurring. Turning off a noisy alarm by getting out of bed is an example.

5. Define and Provide Examples of Schedules of Reinforcement

Schedules of reinforcement determine when and how often reinforcement is delivered. Examples include fixed-ratio (reinforcement after a fixed number of responses), variable-ratio (reinforcement after a variable number of responses), fixed-interval (reinforcement after a fixed time interval), and variable-interval (reinforcement after a variable time interval) schedules.

6. Define and Provide Examples of Positive and Negative Punishment Contingencies

Positive Punishment: Positive punishment involves presenting an aversive stimulus following a behavior to decrease the likelihood of that behavior happening again. Giving a time-out for misbehavior is an example.

Negative Punishment: Negative punishment entails removing a desirable stimulus following a behavior, also to decrease the likelihood of that behavior recurring. Taking away a child's favorite toy for misbehavior is an example.

7. Define and Provide Examples of Automatic and Socially Mediated Contingencies

Automatic Contingency: Automatic contingencies are those where the consequences of behavior are a direct result of the behavior itself, without the involvement of another person. For example, the pain experienced after touching a hot stove is an automatic consequence.

Socially Mediated Contingency: Socially mediated contingencies involve the influence of others' behavior as part of the consequence. When a child receives attention from parents after tantrum behavior, it's a socially mediated contingency.

8. Define and Provide Examples of Unconditioned, Conditioned, and Generalized Reinforcers and Punishers

Unconditioned Reinforcer/Punisher: Unconditioned reinforcers or punishers are inherently reinforcing or punishing and do not require prior learning. Examples include food (reinforcer) and pain (punisher).

Conditioned Reinforcer/Punisher: Conditioned reinforcers or punishers acquire their value through association with other reinforcers or punishers. Money, for example, is a conditioned reinforcer due to its association with obtaining goods and services.

Generalized Reinforcer/Punisher: Generalized reinforcers or punishers are stimuli that can be exchanged for a wide range of other reinforcers or punishers. Money, for instance, is a generalized reinforcer.

9. Define and Provide Examples of Operant Extinction

Operant extinction involves the withholding of reinforcement previously provided for a behavior, resulting in a decrease in the frequency of that behavior. For example, if a child no longer receives attention for tantrums, the tantrum behavior may decrease through extinction.

10. Define and Provide Examples of Stimulus Control

Stimulus control refers to the influence of antecedent stimuli on behavior, indicating that certain behaviors are more likely to occur in the presence of specific stimuli. For instance, a teacher's instruction (antecedent stimulus) may lead to a student's engagement in math problem-solving behavior.

11. Define and Provide Examples of Discrimination, Generalization, and Maintenance

Discrimination: Discrimination is the ability to respond differently to different stimuli or situations. For example, a dog sits when the owner says "sit" but not when a friend uses the same command.

Generalization: Generalization occurs when a behavior learned in one situation carries over to other similar situations or settings. A child who learns to say "please" at home might also use the same polite language at school.

Maintenance: Maintenance refers to the persistence of a behavior over time, even after the initial intervention or training has ended. A child continues to use good manners (saying "please" and "thank you") months after being initially taught these behaviors.

III. Measurement, Data Display, and Interpretation

1. Establish Operational Definitions of Behavior

Operational definitions provide clear and specific descriptions of behaviors to ensure they are observable and measurable. For example, defining "aggression" as "hitting, biting, or kicking."

2. Distinguish Among Direct, Indirect, and Product Measures of Behavior

Direct Measures: Direct measures involve observing and recording behavior as it occurs, such as a teacher noting a student's on-task behavior during class.

Indirect Measures: Indirect measures rely on reports or information from others, such as self-report surveys about one's study habits.

Product Measures: Product measures involve assessing the outcomes or products of behavior, such as evaluating the quality of a completed project.

3. Measure Occurrence (E.g., Frequency, Rate, Percentage)

Frequency: Frequency measures how often a behavior occurs in a specific time period (e.g., 5 tantrums in 30 minutes).

Rate: Rate is the frequency of behavior per unit of time (e.g., 2 tantrums per hour).

Percentage: Percentage measures the proportion of a behavior relative to the total number of opportunities (e.g., completing 80% of assigned tasks).

4. Measure Temporal Dimensions of Behavior (E.g., Duration, Latency, Inter-Response Time)

Duration: Duration measures the length of time a behavior persists (e.g., a 5-minute tantrum).

Latency: Latency measures the time between the presentation of an antecedent and the initiation of the behavior (e.g., 2 minutes from being asked to starting homework).

Inter-Response Time: Inter-response time measures the time between occurrences of the same behavior (e.g., 10 seconds between instances of hand-flapping).

5. Measure Form and Strength of Behavior (E.g., Topography, Magnitude)

Topography: Topography measures the physical form or shape of a behavior, such as the specific movements involved in hand-flapping.

Magnitude: Magnitude measures the force or intensity of a behavior, such as the loudness of vocal outbursts.

6. Measure Trials to Criterion

Trials to criterion involve determining the number of trials or attempts required for a behavior to meet a specific performance standard, such as the number of practice sessions needed for a student to correctly solve math problems.

7. Design and Implement Sampling Procedures (E.g., Interval Recording, Time Sampling)

Sampling procedures involve collecting data at specific intervals, such as interval recording (recording behavior during pre-determined time intervals) or time sampling (sampling behavior at specific moments).

8. Evaluate the Validity and Reliability of Measurement Procedures

Valid measurement procedures accurately assess the intended behavior, while reliable procedures produce consistent results across different observers and occasions. For example, two different observers should record similar observations of the same behavior.

9. Select a Measurement System to Obtain Representative Data Given the Dimensions of Behavior and the Logistics of Observing and Recording

The choice of measurement system depends on the specific behavior and context. For example, if measuring duration of tantrums in a classroom, a combination of interval recording and direct observation may be most suitable.

10. Graph Data to Communicate Relevant Quantitative Relations (E.g., Equal-Interval Graphs, Bar Graphs, Cumulative Records)

Graphing data visually represents behavior change over time, making it easier to understand and communicate. Equal-interval graphs, bar graphs, and cumulative records are common methods for graphing behavioral data.

11. Interpret Graphed Data

Interpreting graphed data involves analyzing the patterns and trends in the data, identifying whether interventions are effective, and making informed decisions for further treatment or intervention adjustments.

Understanding and applying these concepts and principles, as well as mastering the skills of measurement, data display, and interpretation, are essential for effective practice in Applied Behavior Analysis. These elements serve as the backbone of behavior analysis and guide the development of interventions to address a wide range of behavioral challenges.

Chapter 4: Experimental Design

In this chapter, we will delve into the essential aspects of experimental design in the context of Applied Behavior Analysis (ABA). Effective experimental design is crucial for conducting meaningful and rigorous research to understand and modify behavior. We will cover various concepts and methodologies related to experimental design.

1. Distinguish Between Dependent and Independent Variables

Dependent Variable: The dependent variable is the variable that is being observed and measured in an experiment. It represents the outcome or effect you want to study. In ABA, this is often the behavior that you are trying to change.

Independent Variable: The independent variable is the variable that is manipulated or controlled in an experiment to see if it has an effect on the dependent variable. In ABA, this is typically the intervention or treatment used to modify behavior.

2. Distinguish Between Internal and External Validity

Internal Validity: Internal validity refers to the extent to which a study's design allows for conclusions about a cause-and-effect relationship between the independent and dependent variables. It focuses on whether the observed changes in the dependent variable can be attributed to the manipulation of the independent variable and not other factors.

External Validity: External validity refers to the extent to which the results of a study can be generalized to other people, settings, and times. It assesses the extent to which the findings can be applied beyond the specific conditions of the study.

3. Identify the Defining Features of Single-Subject Experimental Designs

Single-Subject Experimental Designs (SSEDs) are research designs where individual subjects serve as their own controls. The defining features of SSEDs include:

Repeated Measures: SSEDs involve measuring the dependent variable repeatedly over time to assess changes.

Prediction: A clear prediction is made about the expected impact of the independent variable on the dependent variable.

Verification: Verification involves systematically demonstrating that changes in the dependent variable are due to the manipulation of the independent variable.

Replication: SSEDs emphasize the replication of experimental conditions to ensure consistency in the results.

4. Describe the Advantages of Single-Subject Experimental Designs Compared to Group Designs

Advantages of SSEDs compared to group designs include:

Precision: SSEDs allow for a detailed analysis of individual behavior, leading to more precise conclusions.

Individualization: Interventions can be tailored to the specific needs of each individual.

Analysis of Trends: SSEDs allow for the analysis of trends and patterns within an individual's behavior.

5. Use Single-Subject Experimental Designs

There are several types of SSEDs, including:

Reversal Design: This involves repeatedly introducing and withdrawing an intervention to assess its effect on behavior.

Multiple Baseline Design: This design involves measuring the behavior of multiple individuals or behaviors in different settings, with interventions introduced at different times.

Multielement Design: In this design, different interventions are introduced simultaneously and compared to see which is the most effective.

Changing Criterion Design: Behavior is reinforced or evaluated against changing criteria to shape the desired behavior.

6. Describe Rationales for Conducting Comparative, Component, and Parametric Analyses

Comparative Analysis: Comparative analysis involves comparing two or more interventions to determine which is the most effective in achieving the desired behavior change.

Component Analysis: Component analysis is used to examine the individual components or elements of an intervention to identify which part is responsible for behavior change.

Parametric Analysis: Parametric analysis explores the impact of varying specific intervention parameters, such as the amount or schedule of reinforcement, to identify the most effective conditions for behavior change.

Effective experimental design is crucial in ABA, as it allows for the systematic investigation and modification of behavior. Single-subject experimental designs, in particular, offer a powerful tool for understanding and shaping behavior in a highly individualized manner. By carefully considering the variables, validity, and design elements discussed in this chapter, ABA practitioners can develop effective interventions to improve the lives of individuals they work with.

Chapter 5: Ethics

Ethics serve as the moral compass that guides the field of Applied Behavior Analysis (ABA). This chapter explores the foundational principles and responsibilities of ethical behavior in ABA. It delves into the ethical considerations that ABA practitioners must adhere to in their professional practice, including their responsibility to clients, stakeholders, supervisees, and the broader public. This chapter aims to provide a comprehensive understanding of the ethical landscape that governs the practice of ABA.

Responsibility as a Professional

ABA practitioners are bound by a set of ethical guidelines that define their professional responsibilities. These guidelines help ensure that the highest standards of care and ethical conduct are maintained. Some key responsibilities as a professional in ABA include:

1. Upholding Ethical Standards

ABA practitioners are ethically obligated to follow the guidelines established by the Behavior Analyst Certification Board (BACB). These standards encompass various areas, such as client confidentiality, informed consent, and competence in practice.

2. Competence and Professional Development

Practitioners must continually strive for professional growth and development. This involves staying updated on the latest research, best practices, and interventions within the field of ABA. They should also seek ongoing training and education to enhance their skills and knowledge.

3. Avoiding Harm

Practitioners have a duty to avoid causing harm to their clients, including physical, emotional, or psychological harm. Ethical considerations require that interventions are designed with the well-being of the client in mind, and any potential risks are minimized.

4. Informed Consent

Informed consent is a fundamental ethical principle. Practitioners must provide clients or their legal guardians with all relevant information regarding the nature, purpose, and potential risks of interventions. Clients should have a clear understanding of what they are consenting to, and they have the right to withdraw consent at any time.

Responsibility in Practice

The ethical responsibilities of ABA practitioners extend to their daily practice. This section outlines key aspects of responsibility in practice, including client welfare, data collection and privacy, and maintaining objectivity.

5. Responsibility to Client Welfare

ABA practitioners have a primary responsibility to ensure the well-being of their clients. This includes developing interventions that are in the best interest of the client, monitoring the impact of interventions on the client's behavior and well-being, and making necessary adjustments to treatment plans.

6. Data Collection and Privacy

Data collection is a critical component of ABA practice. Practitioners must collect data accurately and maintain client confidentiality. This involves securely storing and transmitting client data, only sharing information with authorized individuals, and obtaining proper consent for data sharing.

7. Maintaining Objectivity

Practitioners are responsible for maintaining objectivity and avoiding conflicts of interest in their professional practice. This includes refraining from dual relationships that may compromise their objectivity and professional judgment. Objectivity is crucial for providing unbiased and effective interventions.

Responsibility to Clients and Stakeholders

ABA practitioners have a responsibility to their clients and the various stakeholders involved in the therapeutic process. This includes maintaining transparency, ensuring the rights of clients, and addressing conflicts of interest.

8. Transparency and Collaboration

Practitioners should maintain open and transparent communication with clients and their families. This involves sharing relevant information about the client's progress, the goals of intervention, and the methods being used. Collaboration with other professionals involved in the client's care is also essential for achieving the best outcomes.

9. Protection of Client Rights

ABA practitioners must safeguard the rights and dignity of their clients. This includes respecting the client's autonomy, ensuring their right to make choices when appropriate, and seeking informed consent for interventions.

10. Addressing Conflicts of Interest

Conflicts of interest can arise when ABA practitioners have competing interests that may compromise their ability to act in the best interest of the client. Practitioners have an ethical responsibility to identify and address these conflicts, putting the client's welfare above all other considerations.

Responsibility to Supervisees and Trainees

Ethical responsibilities extend beyond the practitioner-client relationship to include supervising and training new professionals in ABA. This section focuses on the ethical obligations involved in mentorship and training.

11. Supervision and Training

Supervisors have an ethical duty to provide effective supervision and training to their supervisees and trainees. This includes ensuring that they have the knowledge and skills necessary to practice ethically and effectively. Supervisors must also provide feedback and guidance to help their supervisees grow in their professional roles.

12. Ensuring Competence

Supervisors must assess the competence of their supervisees and trainees and provide necessary support and training to address any deficiencies. They should ensure that those under their supervision are capable of delivering safe and effective ABA services.

Responsibility in Public Statements

Public statements made by ABA practitioners can impact the reputation of the field and the well-being of clients. This section addresses the ethical considerations related to public statements and communication.

13. Accurate Representation

Practitioners must accurately represent their qualifications, expertise, and the effectiveness of ABA interventions in public statements. This involves avoiding exaggerated claims and providing clear, evidence-based information to the public.

14. Protection of Confidentiality

Practitioners must take measures to protect the confidentiality of their clients when making public statements. They should avoid disclosing any identifying or sensitive information without proper consent.

Responsibility in Research

Ethical considerations in research are paramount to maintain the integrity of the field and protect the rights of participants. This section discusses the ethical responsibilities of ABA practitioners in research.

15. Ethical Research Conduct

ABA practitioners involved in research must adhere to strict ethical guidelines. This includes obtaining informed consent from research participants, ensuring their well-being, and minimizing any potential harm associated with the research.

16. Transparent Reporting

Practitioners have a responsibility to report research findings accurately and transparently, even if the results do not align with their initial hypotheses or expectations. This helps prevent the dissemination of biased or misleading information.

Ethical considerations are at the core of ABA practice. ABA practitioners must continuously uphold the highest ethical standards in their work to protect the welfare of their clients, maintain the integrity of the field, and contribute to positive, lasting behavior change. Adherence to ethical principles not only ensures the well-being of clients but also sustains the credibility and trustworthiness of ABA as a science and profession.

Chapter 6: Behavior Assessment

Behavior assessment is a foundational step in the field of Applied Behavior Analysis (ABA). It involves a systematic and comprehensive evaluation of an individual's behavior to understand the underlying causes, functions, and contributing factors. This chapter provides an in-depth exploration of the various components of behavior assessment, including reviewing records, determining the need for ABA services, setting behavior-change goals, assessing skill strengths and deficits, conducting preference assessments, identifying the functions of problem behavior, and performing descriptive and functional assessments.

1. Review Records and Available Data at the Outset of the Case

Before commencing any behavior assessment, it is crucial to gather and review all available records and data pertaining to the individual. This historical information can include educational, medical, and previous behavior intervention records. Reviewing this data provides a foundational understanding of the individual's history, challenges, and any past interventions that may have been attempted. It can guide the development of assessment strategies and inform the selection of appropriate interventions.

2. Determine the Need for Behavior-Analytic Services

The determination of the need for behavior-analytic services is a critical step in behavior assessment. This requires an initial evaluation of the individual's situation to assess whether ABA services are appropriate and necessary. Factors that might lead to the need for behavior-analytic services include the presence of problem behavior that interferes with the individual's daily life, limited or impaired communication skills, and other challenging behaviors that impact the individual's well-being and social participation. Identifying the need for ABA services is essential for targeting and addressing specific behavior-change goals.

3. Identify and Prioritize Socially Significant Behavior-Change Goals

Socially significant behavior-change goals are the behaviors that, when targeted for intervention, will have the most meaningful impact on the individual's life. These goals are identified through collaboration with the individual, their caregivers, and relevant stakeholders. Prioritization ensures that interventions are focused on the most crucial areas. Examples of socially significant goals may include improving communication, increasing daily living skills, reducing problem behaviors, and enhancing social interactions.

4. Conduct Assessments of Relevant Skill Strengths and Deficits

To address socially significant behavior-change goals effectively, it is essential to assess the individual's existing skill strengths and deficits. This assessment involves systematically evaluating the individual's abilities across various domains, such as communication, social, daily living, and academic skills. Identifying areas of strength can be leveraged to support skill acquisition, while identifying deficits helps determine where intervention is needed.

5. Conduct Stimulus Preference Assessments (SPA)

Stimulus preference assessments are conducted to identify stimuli that are motivating and reinforcing for the individual. Understanding an individual's preferences is crucial for developing effective reinforcement-based interventions. Preference assessments can take various forms, such as single-item, paired-choice, or multiple-stimulus assessments. The results of these assessments guide the selection of reinforcers to use in behavior intervention plans.

6. Describe the Common Functions of Problem Behavior

Problem behavior serves specific functions or purposes for the individual. Common functions of problem behavior include escape or avoidance of undesired situations, access to attention or tangible items, sensory stimulation or self-stimulation, and communication of needs or desires. Identifying the function of problem behavior is a fundamental step in designing effective behavior interventions, as it informs the selection of appropriate strategies and reinforcers.

7. Conduct a Descriptive Assessment of Problem Behavior

A descriptive assessment, often referred to as indirect assessment, involves gathering information about the antecedents, consequences, and patterns of problem behavior through observation and interviews with caregivers and individuals. This assessment helps in developing a hypothesis about the possible functions of the behavior. It can provide valuable insights into the conditions and triggers that evoke or maintain problem behavior.

8. Conduct a Functional Analysis of Problem Behavior

Functional analysis is the gold standard for identifying the function of problem behavior. It involves manipulating antecedent and consequent variables in controlled settings to determine the function of the behavior. Functional analysis typically includes conditions designed to test for escape, attention, tangible reinforcement, and sensory stimulation functions. The results of the functional analysis provide critical information for designing behavior intervention plans.

9. Interpret Functional Assessment Data

Interpreting functional assessment data involves analyzing the results of both descriptive and functional assessments to develop a comprehensive understanding of the problem behavior. This interpretation informs the selection of interventions that specifically target the function of the behavior. It may lead to the development of a behavior support plan that includes antecedent manipulations, alternative communication strategies, and reinforcement-based interventions designed to address the identified function.

The Integration of Assessment Data

Effective behavior assessment requires the integration of data from various assessment procedures to create a holistic picture of the individual's behavior. It is not uncommon for multiple assessment methods to be used in combination to gain a complete understanding of the individual's strengths, needs, preferences, and the functions of their behavior. The assessment data are the foundation for designing and implementing behavior intervention plans that promote positive behavior change, skill acquisition, and the overall well-being of the individual.

In summary, behavior assessment is a complex and multifaceted process that involves reviewing historical data, identifying the need for ABA services, setting socially significant behavior-change goals, assessing skill strengths and deficits, determining stimulus preferences, understanding the functions of problem behavior, and conducting descriptive and functional assessments. By following a systematic and data-driven approach to behavior assessment, ABA practitioners can develop effective behavior intervention plans that lead to meaningful improvements in the lives of individuals they work with.

Chapter 7: Behavior-Change Procedures

Behavior-change procedures are the heart of Applied Behavior Analysis (ABA) and serve as the cornerstone of effective interventions. In this chapter, we will delve into various behavior-change procedures used in ABA to strengthen, weaken, and modify behavior. These procedures encompass a wide range of strategies that can be tailored to meet the unique needs of individuals, taking into account their specific challenges and goals.

1. Use Positive and Negative Reinforcement Procedures to Strengthen Behavior

Positive Reinforcement:

Positive reinforcement involves presenting a desirable stimulus immediately following a behavior to increase the likelihood of that behavior recurring. For example, giving a child a favorite toy for completing their homework reinforces the homework behavior.

Negative Reinforcement:

Negative reinforcement involves the removal or avoidance of an aversive stimulus to strengthen a behavior. For instance, a seatbelt alarm is turned off when a driver fastens their seatbelt, reinforcing the seatbelt-wearing behavior.

2. Use Interventions Based on Motivating Operations and Discriminative Stimuli

Motivating Operations (MOs):

MOs are environmental variables that alter the value or effectiveness of consequences as reinforcers or punishers. For example, hunger serves as a motivating operation to increase the value of food as a reinforcer.

Discriminative Stimuli (SDs):

SDs are cues or signals that indicate the availability of reinforcement for specific behaviors. When a traffic light turns green, it functions as an SD signaling that it's time to go, reinforcing the behavior of pressing the accelerator pedal.

3. Establish and Use Conditioned Reinforcers (AKA: Secondary Reinforcers)

Conditioned reinforcers are initially neutral stimuli that acquire reinforcing properties through association with primary reinforcers. For instance, praise becomes a conditioned reinforcer when consistently paired with the primary reinforcer of food.

4. Use Stimulus and Response Prompts and Fading

Stimulus Prompts:

Stimulus prompts involve providing additional cues or hints to assist an individual in performing a target behavior. Gradual fading of these prompts helps the individual learn the behavior independently.

Response Prompts:

Response prompts are physical or verbal cues provided to guide an individual's behavior. Over time, these prompts are reduced to encourage independent performance.

5. Use Modeling and Imitation Training

Modeling involves demonstrating a behavior for an individual to observe and imitate. Imitation training is the process of teaching individuals to replicate the demonstrated behavior. Both are effective for skill acquisition.

6. Use Instructions and Rules

Instructions and rules provide clear guidance to individuals regarding what behavior is expected or required. They are often used in educational and workplace settings to facilitate appropriate behavior.

7. Use Shaping

Shaping involves reinforcing successive approximations of a target behavior until the desired behavior is achieved. This method is particularly useful for teaching complex behaviors in incremental steps.

8. Use Chaining

Chaining is a technique for teaching a sequence of behaviors in a specific order. Each step in the sequence is reinforced until the individual can complete the entire chain.

9. Use Discrete-Trial, Free-Operant, and Naturalistic Teaching Arrangements

Discrete-Trial Teaching:

In discrete-trial teaching, skills are taught in a structured and controlled environment. Each trial presents a specific antecedent, followed by a behavior, and then a consequence.

Free-Operant Teaching:

Free-operant teaching involves teaching skills in a less structured, more natural setting, allowing individuals to engage in behaviors at their own pace.

Naturalistic Teaching:

Naturalistic teaching incorporates skills into everyday, real-life situations, facilitating skill generalization and promoting functional behavior.

10. Teach Simple and Conditional Discriminations

Simple discriminations involve recognizing one antecedent as signaling reinforcement, while another signals non-reinforcement. Conditional discriminations extend this concept, allowing individuals to respond appropriately to a variety of cues and contingencies.

11. Use Skinner's Analysis to Teach Verbal Behavior

Skinner's analysis of verbal behavior, known as the analysis of verbal operants, provides a framework for understanding and teaching language and communication skills. It includes concepts like manding (requesting) and tacting (labeling).

12. Use Equivalence-Based Instruction

Equivalence-based instruction is a teaching approach that fosters the emergence of relations between stimuli, enabling individuals to make novel responses based on previously learned relationships.

13. Use the High-Probability Instructional Sequence

The high-probability instructional sequence involves interspersing high-probability or easy tasks with low-probability or difficult tasks to increase compliance and task engagement.

14. Use Reinforcement Procedures to Weaken Behavior (E.g., DRA, FCT, DRO, DRL, NCR)

Differential Reinforcement of Alternative Behavior (DRA):

DRA involves reinforcing an alternative, more appropriate behavior while withholding reinforcement for problem behavior.

Functional Communication Training (FCT):

FCT focuses on teaching individuals to use appropriate communication to replace problem behavior.

Differential Reinforcement of Other Behavior (DRO):

DRO involves reinforcing any behavior other than the target problem behavior, which serves to reduce the occurrence of the problem behavior.

Differential Reinforcement of Low Rates (DRL):

DRL reinforces behavior when it occurs at a lower rate than a predetermined criterion, which helps reduce excessive behavior.

Noncontingent Reinforcement (NCR):

NCR provides reinforcement on a fixed schedule, regardless of the individual's behavior, as a way to decrease the motivation to engage in problem behavior.

15. Use Extinction (AKA: Operant Extinction)

Extinction involves discontinuing reinforcement for a previously reinforced behavior. This procedure aims to reduce the occurrence of problem behavior. It is crucial to ensure consistency in the absence of reinforcement.

16. Use Positive and Negative Punishment (E.g., Time-Out, Response Cost, Overcorrection)

Time-Out:

Time-out involves removing access to positive reinforcement following problem behavior. It can be implemented in various forms, such as exclusionary or non-exclusionary time-out.

Response Cost:

Response cost involves the removal of a specific reinforcer contingent on problem behavior. For instance, a fine may be imposed for tardiness.

Overcorrection:

Overcorrection requires an individual to engage in an effortful, corrective behavior to address the consequences of their problem behavior. This may include restitution and positive practice.

17. Use Token Economies (AKA: Token System)

Token economies involve a system in which individuals earn tokens for engaging in appropriate behavior. These tokens can be exchanged for desired reinforcers.

18. Use Group Contingencies

Group contingencies involve providing reinforcement or consequences to a group of individuals based on their collective behavior. Examples include the Good Behavior Game in a classroom setting.

19. Use Contingency Contracting (AKA: Behavioral Contract)

Contingency contracting involves creating a written agreement specifying the terms and conditions for earning reinforcement based on the individual's behavior.

20. Use Self-Management Strategies

Self-management strategies empower individuals to monitor and control their own behavior. These strategies may include self-monitoring, self-reinforcement, and self-prompting.

21. Use Procedures to Promote Stimulus and Response Generalization

Generalization procedures are employed to ensure that learned skills are applied across various settings, people, and materials. This helps individuals generalize their behavior-change across different situations.

22. Use Procedures to Promote Maintenance (AKA: Response Maintenance)

Maintenance procedures are designed to sustain the behavior change over time. These may include intermittent reinforcement schedules and periodic review and practice of skills.

Behavior-change procedures in ABA encompass a wide range of strategies to strengthen, weaken, and modify behavior. These procedures are tailored to meet individual needs and goals, making ABA a highly flexible and effective approach for improving the behavior and quality of life for those it serves. ABA practitioners carefully select and implement these procedures to create personalized intervention plans that address each individual's unique challenges and opportunities for growth.

Chapter 8: Personnel Supervision and Management

Personnel supervision and management are essential components of maintaining the quality and effectiveness of behavior-analytic services. This chapter explores the reasons for using behavior-analytic supervision, the potential risks of ineffective supervision, and the key principles and practices involved in effectively supervising behavior analysts.

1. State the Reasons for Using Behavior-Analytic Supervision and the Potential Risks of Ineffective Supervision

Reasons for Behavior-Analytic Supervision:

Behavior-analytic supervision is essential for several reasons:

Maintaining Quality Assurance: Supervision ensures that behavior-analytic services are delivered with precision, adhering to ethical and clinical standards.

Skill Development: It facilitates the growth and development of supervisees' behavior-analytic skills, contributing to their professional competence.

Client Welfare: Effective supervision directly impacts client outcomes, ensuring the delivery of evidence-based, effective interventions.

Ethical Adherence: Supervision assists in upholding ethical guidelines, such as maintaining client confidentiality and informed consent.

Potential Risks of Ineffective Supervision:

Ineffective supervision can result in a range of negative consequences:

Poor Client Outcomes: Clients may receive suboptimal or ineffective interventions, impacting their progress and well-being.

Poor Supervisee Performance: Supervisees may not develop the necessary skills, leading to inadequate service provision.

Ethical Violations: Inadequate supervision can lead to ethical breaches, such as privacy violations or unprofessional conduct.

Reduced Professionalism: Ineffective supervision may hinder the professional development of behavior analysts.

2. Establish Clear Performance Expectations for the Supervisor and Supervisee

Clear performance expectations are fundamental to successful supervision. Both the supervisor and supervisee should understand their respective roles and responsibilities. Expectations should be outlined in terms of supervision processes, goals, timelines, and evaluation criteria. This clarity ensures that the supervision relationship is productive and efficient.

3. Select Supervision Goals Based on an Assessment of the Supervisee's Skills

Supervision goals should be individualized based on the supervisee's current skill level, strengths, and areas needing improvement. A skills assessment, such as the Competency Assessment, can help determine the specific goals for each supervisee. Supervision goals should align with professional development and competence.

4. Train Personnel to Competently Perform Assessment and Intervention Procedures

Effective supervision involves training supervisees to competently conduct assessments and interventions. This may include hands-on training, modeling, and guidance to ensure that supervisees can independently execute these procedures. Supervisees should be well-versed in assessment tools, data collection, and behavior-change strategies.

5. Use Performance Monitoring, Feedback, and Reinforcement Systems

Performance monitoring involves systematically tracking supervisee progress toward supervision goals. Regular feedback is essential to inform supervisees of their performance, both areas of strength and areas needing improvement. Reinforcement systems can be implemented to motivate and reward competent and ethical behavior-analytic practice.

6. Use a Functional Assessment Approach (E.g., Performance Diagnostics) to Identify Variables Affecting Personnel Performance

Supervisors should use a functional assessment approach to understand the variables impacting personnel performance. This includes identifying environmental factors, motivational variables, and skill deficits that may influence performance. A functional assessment enables supervisors to pinpoint areas requiring support and intervention.

7. Use Function-Based Strategies to Improve Personnel Performance

Once the variables affecting personnel performance are identified, function-based strategies can be employed to improve performance. This may involve antecedent manipulations, reinforcement strategies, or skill-building programs designed to address identified deficits.

8. Evaluate the Effects of Supervision (E.g., on Client Outcomes, on Supervisee Repertoires)

Supervision's effectiveness should be regularly assessed. This includes evaluating its impact on client outcomes to ensure that services are improving or maintaining client welfare. Additionally, the development and maintenance of supervisee repertoires should be monitored to confirm that supervision goals are being met.

Personnel supervision and management are integral to the practice of behavior analysis. Effective supervision supports the growth and professional development of behavior analysts, ensuring the delivery of high-quality services and ethical conduct. By adhering to clear performance expectations, conducting assessments, and employing function-based strategies, behavior-analytic supervision can optimize both client outcomes and the professional growth of supervisees. Evaluating the impact of supervision reinforces its role in maintaining the integrity of behavior-analytic services.

Chapter 9: Practice Questions and Answers

1. When a behavior analyst conducts multiple tests of her therapy before writing it in a formal behavior program, she is sticking to which basic assumption of behavior analysis?

A. Determination

B. The Parsimony Law

C. Empiricism

D. None of the preceding

Answer: C

Explanation: Behavior analysts adhere to the basic assumption of empiricism, which emphasizes the importance of data-driven decision-making. Conducting multiple tests before implementing a therapy program ensures that interventions are based on empirical evidence and are likely to be effective.

2. In behavior analysis, the term "operant" refers to which type of behavior?

A. Involuntary reflexes

B. Reflexive behaviors

C. Voluntary behaviors influenced by their consequences

D. Innate behaviors

Answer: C

Explanation: Operant behaviors are voluntary actions that are influenced by their consequences, in contrast to reflexive, involuntary behaviors.

3. What is the primary function of a discriminative stimulus (SD) in behavior analysis?

A. It reinforces behavior.

B. It signals when a behavior should occur to be reinforced.

C. It extinguishes behavior.

D. It punishes behavior.

Answer: B

Explanation: A discriminative stimulus (SD) signals when a behavior should occur to be reinforced, essentially indicating that reinforcement is available for the behavior under specific conditions.

4. A behavior analyst is conducting a preference assessment. What is the goal of this assessment?

A. To identify preferred reinforcers for an individual

B. To identify aversive stimuli for behavior reduction

C. To assess the individual's intelligence

D. To evaluate motor skills

Answer: A

Explanation: The primary goal of a preference assessment is to identify preferred reinforcers or stimuli for an individual. This information is crucial for effective behavior-change programs.

5. In behavior analysis, what is the term for the phenomenon where a behavior that was previously reinforced no longer produces reinforcement and decreases in frequency?

A. Extinction

B. Generalization

C. Discrimination

D. Reinforcement

Answer: A

Explanation: Extinction is the process by which a previously reinforced behavior decreases in frequency when reinforcement is no longer provided for that behavior.

6. What is the term for the process of reinforcing successive approximations of a target behavior until the desired behavior is achieved?

A. Shaping

B. Chaining

C. Modeling

D. Generalization

Answer: A

Explanation: Shaping is the process of reinforcing successive approximations of a behavior to guide an individual toward the desired behavior.

7. When a behavior analyst uses a functional analysis to determine the antecedents and consequences that maintain problem behavior, they are seeking to identify the behavior's:

A. Dimensions

B. Functions

C. Intensity

D. Duration

Answer: B

Explanation: In a functional analysis, behavior analysts seek to identify the functions or purposes that maintain problem behavior, such as escape, attention, or access to tangible items.

8. What term is used to describe a reinforcement schedule where reinforcement is delivered after a fixed number of responses?

A. Fixed-Interval Schedule

B. Variable-Ratio Schedule

C. Fixed-Ratio Schedule

D. Variable-Interval Schedule

Answer: C

Explanation: In a fixed-ratio schedule, reinforcement is delivered after a fixed number of responses. For example, every fifth correct response is reinforced.

9. A behavior analyst is teaching a child to say "please" when requesting an item, instead of grabbing or pointing. This is an example of:

A. Shaping

B. Modeling

C. Discrimination training

D. Extinction

Answer: A

Explanation: Shaping is the process of reinforcing successive approximations of a target behavior. In this case, the behavior analyst is reinforcing the child's approximation toward saying "please" instead of grabbing or pointing.

10. What is the primary function of a behavior intervention plan (BIP)?

- A. To diagnose behavioral disorders

- B. To design and implement a systematic approach to reduce or eliminate problem behaviors

- C. To provide medication to individuals with behavior disorders

- D. To establish normative behaviors

- Answer: B

- Explanation: A behavior intervention plan (BIP) is designed to create a systematic approach for reducing or eliminating problem behaviors and promoting desirable behaviors.

11. Which of the following is an example of negative reinforcement?

- A. A student receives a sticker for answering a question correctly.

- B. A driver fastens their seatbelt to turn off a seatbelt alarm.

- C. A child receives a time-out for hitting another child.

- D. A dog is given a treat for sitting on command.

- Answer: B

- Explanation: Negative reinforcement involves the removal or avoidance of an aversive stimulus to strengthen a behavior. In this case, fastening the seatbelt removes the aversive seatbelt alarm.

12. What does the term "antecedent" refer to in behavior analysis?

- A. A consequence that follows a behavior

- B. A behavior's intensity

- C. A stimulus or event that precedes a behavior and influences its occurrence

- D. A description of the setting in which a behavior occurs

- Answer: C

- Explanation: Antecedents are stimuli or events that precede a behavior and influence the likelihood of that behavior occurring.

13. In ABA, the process of using positive reinforcement to increase a desirable behavior is known as:

- A. Shaping

- B. Negative reinforcement

- C. Extinction

- D. Reinforcement

- Answer: D

- Explanation: Using positive reinforcement to increase a desirable behavior is simply referred to as reinforcement in ABA.

14. What term is used to describe a reinforcement schedule where reinforcement is delivered after a variable number of responses?

- A. Fixed-Ratio Schedule

- B. Variable-Ratio Schedule

- C. Fixed-Interval Schedule

- D. Variable-Interval Schedule

- Answer: B

- Explanation: In a variable-ratio schedule, reinforcement is delivered after a variable number of responses. The variability keeps the behavior active.

15. In ABA, what is the term for a decrease in the frequency of a behavior when reinforcement is no longer provided for that behavior?

- A. Reinforcement

- B. Extinction

- C. Shaping

- D. Chaining

- Answer: B

- Explanation: Extinction refers to the decrease in the frequency of a behavior when reinforcement is no longer provided for that behavior.

16. Which of the following is an example of a conditioned reinforcer?

- A. Food

- B. A smiley face sticker

- C. A glass of water when thirsty

- D. A loud noise

- Answer: B

- Explanation: A conditioned reinforcer is a stimulus that gains its reinforcing properties through association with primary reinforcers. A smiley face sticker, which may be paired with praise or other reinforcers, becomes conditioned.

17. A behavior analyst conducts a functional analysis and determines that a child's aggressive behavior is maintained by escaping academic demands. What type of reinforcement is maintaining this behavior?

- A. Positive reinforcement

- B. Negative reinforcement

- C. Punishment

- D. Extinction

- Answer: B

- Explanation: The aggressive behavior is maintained by escaping academic demands, which is a form of negative reinforcement, as removing the academic demand strengthens the behavior.

18. Which of the following is NOT a dimension of behavior that is typically measured in behavior analysis?

- A. Frequency

- B. Duration

- C. Volume

- D. Latency

- Answer: C

- Explanation: While frequency, duration, and latency are common dimensions of behavior measured in behavior analysis, "volume" is not typically used as a dimension in this context.

19. In a discrete-trial teaching arrangement, what happens immediately after the presentation of a discriminative stimulus (SD)?

- A. The child is placed in time-out.

- B. The child responds, and the response is followed by a consequence.

- C. The child is praised for good behavior.

- D. The session ends.

- Answer: B

- Explanation: In discrete-trial teaching, the child responds to the discriminative stimulus (SD), and their response is followed by a consequence (e.g., reinforcement or feedback).

20. A child's problem behavior decreases when they no longer receive attention for engaging in that behavior. What behavior-change procedure is this an example of?

- A. Negative reinforcement

- B. Positive reinforcement

- C. Extinction

- D. Punishment

- Answer: C

- Explanation: In this scenario, the problem behavior decreases because attention is no longer provided (extinction). The removal of attention serves as the extinction procedure.

21. In behavior analysis, the concept of "functional assessment" refers to:

- A. The assessment of an individual's physical health.

- B. Assessing an individual's cognitive abilities.

- C. Identifying the antecedents and consequences that maintain problem behavior.

- D. Measuring the individual's level of motivation.

- Answer: C

- Explanation: Functional assessment in behavior analysis is the process of identifying the antecedents and consequences that maintain problem behavior, helping to determine the function or purpose of the behavior.

22. A behavior analyst is conducting a preference assessment to identify reinforcers for a client. What type of preference assessment involves presenting a set of items and allowing the client to choose their preferred item(s)?

- A. Paired-choice preference assessment

- B. Single-item preference assessment

- C. Multiple-stimulus without replacement preference assessment

- D. Reinforcer assessment

- Answer: A

- Explanation: A paired-choice preference assessment involves presenting pairs of items and allowing the client to choose between them, identifying preferred items.

23. What is a "functional analysis" in behavior analysis used for?

- A. To determine the function or purpose of a behavior

- B. To evaluate academic achievement

- C. To diagnose psychological disorders

- D. To assess general intelligence

- Answer: A

- Explanation: A functional analysis is used to determine the function or purpose of a behavior, such as identifying whether the behavior is maintained by attention, escape, access to tangible items, or automatic reinforcement.

24. A behavior analyst is conducting a functional analysis and finds that a client's self-injurious behavior is maintained by the attention it receives from caregivers. What function of behavior is this indicative of?

- A. Escape

- B. Sensory stimulation

- C. Attention

- D. Access to tangible items

- Answer: C

- Explanation: When self-injurious behavior is maintained by the attention it receives from caregivers, it is indicative of the attention-maintained function of behavior.

25. What is the primary goal of a behavior intervention plan (BIP) in behavior analysis?

- A. To diagnose psychological disorders

- B. To provide medical treatment

- C. To design and implement a systematic approach to reduce or eliminate problem behaviors

- D. To assess academic achievement

- Answer: C

- Explanation: The primary goal of a behavior intervention plan (BIP) is to design and implement a systematic approach for reducing or eliminating problem behaviors and promoting desirable behaviors.

26. In behavior analysis, the term "generalization" refers to:

- A. The use of reinforcement

- B. The application of learned behaviors across different situations and contexts

- C. The use of extinction

- D. The application of punishment

- Answer: B

- Explanation: Generalization in behavior analysis refers to the application of learned behaviors across different situations and contexts, demonstrating the adaptability of those behaviors.

27. What is a "conditioned reinforcer" in behavior analysis?

- A. A stimulus that automatically elicits a response

- B. A previously neutral stimulus that becomes reinforcing through association with other reinforcers

- C. A primary reinforcer

- D. A stimulus used for punishment

- Answer: B

- Explanation: A conditioned reinforcer is a previously neutral stimulus that becomes reinforcing through association with other reinforcers. It acquires its reinforcing properties.

28. What is a "tact" in the context of verbal behavior analysis?

- A. A request for reinforcement

- B. A response to a discriminative stimulus

- C. A label for a nonverbal stimulus in the environment

- D. A verbal behavior targeted for reduction

- Answer: C

- Explanation: In verbal behavior analysis, a "tact" is a verbal response that serves as a label for a nonverbal stimulus in the environment. It is often a description or label of something in the individual's surroundings.

29. What does it mean when a behavior analyst uses the term "reinforcement schedule"?

- A. The analyst's work schedule

- B. A plan for when to provide reinforcement based on specific criteria

- C. The timing of the client's daily activities

- D. A schedule for medical appointments

- Answer: B

- Explanation: A reinforcement schedule is a plan for when to provide reinforcement based on specific criteria, such as continuous reinforcement, fixed-ratio, variable-ratio, fixed-interval, or variable-interval schedules.

30. In behavior analysis, what is a "prompt" used for?

- A. To extinguish behavior

- B. To signal the availability of reinforcement

- C. To provide additional cues or hints to assist an individual in performing a target behavior

- D. To punish behavior

- Answer: C

- Explanation: A prompt is used to provide additional cues or hints to assist an individual in performing a target behavior. It is often used during skill acquisition to guide the individual.

31. When a behavior analyst uses a "token economy," what is the purpose of this system?

- A. To provide a method for diagnosing psychological disorders

- B. To establish normative behaviors

- C. To provide medication to clients

- D. To reinforce appropriate behavior using tokens or points

- Answer: D

- Explanation: A token economy is a system designed to reinforce appropriate behavior using tokens or points, which can be exchanged for desired reinforcers.

32. What term is used to describe a reinforcement schedule where reinforcement is delivered after a fixed amount of time has passed since the last reinforcement?

- A. Fixed-Ratio Schedule

- B. Variable-Interval Schedule

- C. Fixed-Interval Schedule

- D. Variable-Ratio Schedule

- Answer: C

- Explanation: In a fixed-interval schedule, reinforcement is delivered after a fixed amount of time has passed since the last reinforcement. For example, an exam every two weeks.

33. What is "chaining" in the context of behavior analysis?

- A. A process used for assessing environmental variables

- B. A procedure for training individuals to perform a sequence of behaviors in a specific order

- C. A strategy for reinforcing appropriate behavior using tokens

- D. A method for teaching new language skills

- Answer: B

- Explanation: Chaining is a procedure used for training individuals to perform a sequence of behaviors in a specific order, creating a behavioral chain.

34. In behavior analysis, what is a "conditional discrimination"?

- A. Recognizing the function of a behavior

- B. Distinguishing between different stimuli and responding appropriately based on cues

- C. A type of reinforcement schedule

- D. Responding to all stimuli in the same way

- Answer: B

- Explanation: A conditional discrimination involves distinguishing between different stimuli and responding appropriately based on cues or discriminative stimuli.

35. A behavior analyst is using "modeling" as an intervention strategy. What is the purpose of this technique?

- A. To provide reinforcement for appropriate behavior

- B. To provide extinction for inappropriate behavior

- C. To demonstrate a target behavior for the individual to imitate

- D. To conduct a functional analysis

- Answer: C

- Explanation: Modeling is used to demonstrate a target behavior for the individual to imitate or learn from the example.

36. In behavior analysis, the term "discriminative stimulus" (SD) is used to refer to:

- A. A stimulus that is always present in the environment

- B. A stimulus that signals when a behavior should occur to be reinforced

- C. A type of conditioned reinforcer

- D. A stimulus used for punishment

- Answer: B

- Explanation: A discriminative stimulus (SD) signals when a behavior should occur to be reinforced, essentially indicating that reinforcement is available for the behavior under specific conditions.

37. A behavior analyst is conducting an assessment to identify the reinforcers for a client's appropriate behaviors. What type of assessment is this?

- A. Reinforcer assessment

- B. Preference assessment

- C. Functional analysis

- D. Punishment assessment

- Answer: B

- Explanation: A preference assessment is conducted to identify the reinforcers or stimuli that are preferred by a client for use in behavior-change programs.

38. What is a "task analysis" used for in behavior analysis?

- A. To diagnose psychological disorders

- B. To assess an individual's cognitive abilities

- C. To break down complex skills into smaller, teachable units or steps

- D. To assess an individual's physical health

- Answer: C

- Explanation: A task analysis is used to break down complex skills into smaller, teachable units or steps, making it easier to teach and assess an individual's progress.

39. What is the purpose of "negative punishment" in behavior analysis?

- A. To decrease the likelihood of a behavior by removing an aversive stimulus

- B. To increase the likelihood of a behavior by adding a reinforcing stimulus

- C. To decrease the likelihood of a behavior by adding an aversive stimulus

- D. To increase the likelihood of a behavior by removing a reinforcing stimulus

- Answer: A

- Explanation: Negative punishment involves decreasing the likelihood of a behavior by removing a reinforcing stimulus, which serves to decrease the future occurrence of that behavior.

40. In behavior analysis, what is the term for an increase in the frequency of a behavior when reinforcement is provided for a response that is similar but not identical to the target behavior?

- A. Generalization

- B. Discrimination

- C. Extinction

- D. Shaping

- Answer: D

- Explanation: Shaping is the process of reinforcing successive approximations of a target behavior, which involves reinforcing behaviors that are similar but not identical to the desired behavior.

41. A behavior analyst is conducting a trial in which they present a discriminative stimulus (SD) and reinforce the client's response consistently with a reinforcer. What type of reinforcement schedule is this an example of?

- A. Continuous reinforcement

- B. Variable-ratio schedule

- C. Fixed-interval schedule

- D. Variable-interval schedule

- Answer: A

- Explanation: In continuous reinforcement, every correct response is consistently reinforced with a reinforcer.

42. In the context of behavior analysis, what does "DRO" stand for?

- A. Differential Reinforcement of Other behavior

- B. Differential Reinforcement of Negative behavior

- C. Differential Reinforcement of Opposite behavior

- D. Differential Reinforcement of Operant behavior

- Answer: A

- Explanation: DRO stands for Differential Reinforcement of Other behavior, which involves reinforcing behaviors other than the target behavior.

43. A behavior analyst is using "prompt fading" as a teaching strategy. What does this involve?

- A. Gradually removing prompts to promote independent responding

- B. Increasing the intensity of prompts to speed up learning

- C. Using continuous reinforcement for the target behavior

- D. Introducing novel, unrelated stimuli

- Answer: A

- Explanation: Prompt fading involves gradually removing prompts to promote independent responding by the individual.

44. What is the primary goal of "stimulus control" in behavior analysis?

- A. To create a controlled environment with no external stimuli

- B. To weaken the influence of discriminative stimuli on behavior

- C. To strengthen the influence of discriminative stimuli on behavior

- D. To eliminate all stimuli in the environment

- Answer: C

- Explanation: The primary goal of stimulus control is to strengthen the influence of discriminative stimuli on behavior, making the behavior more likely to occur under specific conditions.

45. In behavior analysis, what is a "response class"?

- A. A group of behaviors that result in the same consequence

- B. A category of behaviors that always require punishment

- C. A set of behaviors that are never reinforced

- D. A type of reinforcer

- Answer: A

- Explanation: A response class is a group of behaviors that result in the same consequence or share similar functions. They are treated similarly in behavior analysis.

46. What is the term for the process of decreasing the frequency of a behavior by removing or withholding reinforcement for that behavior?

- A. Reinforcement

- B. Extinction

- C. Shaping

- D. Modeling

- Answer: B

- Explanation: Extinction is the process of decreasing the frequency of a behavior by removing or withholding reinforcement for that behavior.

47. What is a "negative reinforcer" in behavior analysis?

- A. A consequence that strengthens a behavior by adding something desirable

- B. A stimulus that automatically elicits a response

- C. A consequence that strengthens a behavior by removing or avoiding something aversive

- D. A stimulus used for punishment

- Answer: C

- Explanation: A negative reinforcer is a consequence that strengthens a behavior by removing or avoiding something aversive.

48. A behavior analyst is teaching a child to wash their hands independently. What is this an example of?

- A. Chaining

- B. Prompting

- C. Reinforcement

- D. Shaping

- Answer: A

- Explanation: Teaching a child to perform a sequence of behaviors in a specific order, such as washing hands independently, is an example of chaining.

49. In behavior analysis, what does the term "antecedent intervention" refer to?

- A. Intervening before a behavior occurs to prevent it

- B. Intervening after a behavior occurs to reinforce it

- C. Intervening during a behavior to prompt it

- D. Intervening after a behavior occurs to punish it

- Answer: A

- Explanation: Antecedent intervention involves intervening before a behavior occurs to prevent or reduce it.

50. What is the primary function of "positive punishment" in behavior analysis?

- A. To increase the likelihood of a behavior by adding an aversive stimulus

- B. To decrease the likelihood of a behavior by removing a reinforcing stimulus

- C. To decrease the likelihood of a behavior by adding an aversive stimulus

- D. To increase the likelihood of a behavior by removing an aversive stimulus

- Answer: C

- Explanation: Positive punishment involves decreasing the likelihood of a behavior by adding an aversive stimulus, which serves to decrease the future occurrence of that behavior.

51. In behavior analysis, what is a "generalization gradient"?

- A. A measurement of the intensity of reinforcement

- B. A graph showing the decline in behavior over time

- C. A graph showing the spread of a behavior across different situations or stimuli

- D. A measurement of response latency

- Answer: C

- Explanation: A generalization gradient is a graph showing the spread or extent to which a behavior occurs across different situations or stimuli.

52. What is "response latency" in behavior analysis?

- A. The time it takes for a response to occur after a stimulus is presented

- B. The number of responses within a certain time frame

- C. The duration of a response

- D. The intensity of a response

- Answer: A

- Explanation: Response latency is the time it takes for a response to occur after a stimulus is presented.

53. What is a "continuous reinforcement schedule" in behavior analysis?

- A. A schedule where reinforcement is provided intermittently

- B. A schedule where reinforcement is provided for every occurrence of the target behavior

- C. A schedule where reinforcement is provided for only some correct responses

- D. A schedule where reinforcement is provided for responses that are spaced out over time

- Answer: B

- Explanation: In a continuous reinforcement schedule, reinforcement is provided for every occurrence of the target behavior.

54. A behavior analyst is using "prompt hierarchy" as an intervention strategy. What does this involve?

- A. Using a sequence of prompts, from most intrusive to least intrusive, to teach a behavior

- B. Introducing aversive stimuli to decrease a behavior

- C. Reinforcing a behavior consistently

- D. Using differential reinforcement

- Answer: A

- Explanation: A prompt hierarchy involves using a sequence of prompts, from most intrusive to least intrusive, to teach a behavior and then systematically fading the prompts.

55. What is the term for a reinforcement schedule where reinforcement is delivered after a fixed number of responses?

- A. Variable-Ratio Schedule

- B. Fixed-Ratio Schedule

- C. Variable-Interval Schedule

- D. Fixed-Interval Schedule

- Answer: B

- Explanation: In a fixed-ratio schedule, reinforcement is delivered after a fixed number of responses.

56. What does it mean when a behavior analyst uses the term "tangible item" in the context of reinforcement?

- A. An item that can be touched

- B. A reinforcer that is a physical object or activity

- C. An intangible concept

- D. A prompt for behavior

- Answer: B

- Explanation: In the context of reinforcement, a "tangible item" refers to a reinforcer that is a physical object or activity, such as a toy or a preferred food item.

57. What does the term "multielement design" refer to in single-subject research?

- A. A design involving multiple subjects

- B. A design with multiple dependent variables

- C. A design in which multiple behaviors are assessed within the same subject

- D. A design with multiple treatment phases

- Answer: C

- Explanation: In single-subject research, a multielement design involves assessing multiple behaviors within the same subject to compare their effects.

58. In behavior analysis, what is the term for "self-management"?

- A. A process for administering treatment to oneself

- B. A reinforcement procedure used in group settings

- C. A form of conditioning involving peer interactions

- D. A process in which an individual engages in behavior change for themselves

- Answer: D

- Explanation: Self-management in behavior analysis is the process in which an individual engages in behavior change for themselves, including self-monitoring and self-reinforcement.

59. What is a "functional behavior assessment" (FBA) used for in behavior analysis?

- A. To identify the frequency of problem behaviors

- B. To determine the duration of problem behaviors

- C. To identify the antecedents and consequences that maintain problem behaviors

- D. To establish reinforcement schedules

- Answer: C

- Explanation: A functional behavior assessment (FBA) is used to identify the antecedents and consequences that maintain problem behaviors, helping to determine the function or purpose of the behavior.

60. What is the term for a reduction in behavior when reinforcement is no longer provided for that behavior at the same rate?

- A. Reinforcement

- B. Extinction burst

- C. Negative reinforcement

- D. Shaping

- Answer: B

- Explanation: An extinction burst is a temporary increase in the frequency and intensity of the behavior when reinforcement is no longer provided at the same rate.

61. What does "BCBA" stand for in the context of behavior analysis?

- A. Behavior Control and Analysis Board

- B. Board Certified Behavioral Analyst

- C. Behavior Certification and Analysis Board

- D. Board Certified Behavior Analyst

- Answer: D

- Explanation: BCBA stands for Board Certified Behavior Analyst, which is a professional certification in the field of behavior analysis.

62. In behavior analysis, what is a "baseline" used for?

- A. A control condition for assessing the effects of an intervention

- B. A schedule for reinforcement

- C. A form of punishment

- D. A method for data collection

- Answer: A

- Explanation: A baseline is a control condition used for assessing the effects of an intervention by collecting data on the behavior before any treatment is implemented.

63. What is a "negative reinforcer" in behavior analysis?

- A. A stimulus that is aversive to all individuals

- B. A consequence that decreases the likelihood of a behavior

- C. A consequence that strengthens a behavior by adding something desirable

- D. A consequence that strengthens a behavior by removing or avoiding something aversive

- Answer: D

- Explanation: A negative reinforcer is a consequence that strengthens a behavior by removing or avoiding something aversive.

64. What is the term for a reinforcement schedule where reinforcement is delivered after a variable amount of time has passed since the last reinforcement?

- A. Fixed-Interval Schedule

- B. Variable-Interval Schedule

- C. Fixed-Ratio Schedule

- D. Variable-Ratio Schedule

- Answer: B

- Explanation: In a variable-interval schedule, reinforcement is delivered after a variable amount of time has passed since the last reinforcement.

65. What does it mean when a behavior analyst uses the term "discrete-trial teaching"?

- A. Teaching a skill in a continuous, ongoing manner without interruption

- B. Teaching a skill in isolated, structured trials with clear beginning and end

- C. Teaching through modeling only

- D. Teaching through punishment procedures

- Answer: B

- Explanation: Discrete-trial teaching involves teaching a skill in isolated, structured trials with clear beginning and end, often involving a discriminative stimulus, a response, and a consequence.

66. In behavior analysis, what is a "token economy" used for?

- A. To diagnose psychological disorders

- B. To establish a controlled environment with no external stimuli

- C. To provide a method for administering medication

- D. To reinforce appropriate behavior using tokens or points

- Answer: D

- Explanation: A token economy is used to reinforce appropriate behavior using tokens or points, which can be exchanged for desired reinforcers.

67. What is a "rule-governed behavior" in behavior analysis?

- A. Behavior controlled by rules, instructions, or verbal guidance

- B. Behavior that is innate and not learned

- C. Behavior that is solely influenced by environmental stimuli

- D. Behavior that is never reinforced

- Answer: A

- Explanation: Rule-governed behavior is behavior that is controlled by rules, instructions, or verbal guidance rather than direct environmental contingencies.

68. What does "conditional discrimination" involve in behavior analysis?

- A. Responding to all stimuli in the same way

- B. Distinguishing between different stimuli and responding appropriately based on cues

- C. Ignoring all environmental stimuli

- D. Responding only to conditioned reinforcers

- Answer: B

- Explanation: Conditional discrimination involves distinguishing between different stimuli and responding appropriately based on cues or discriminative stimuli.

69. In behavior analysis, what is the term for a stimulus that automatically elicits a response without any prior learning or conditioning?

- A. Conditioned stimulus

- B. Neutral stimulus

- C. Unconditioned stimulus

- D. Discriminative stimulus

- Answer: C

- Explanation: An unconditioned stimulus is a stimulus that automatically elicits a response without any prior learning or conditioning.

70. What is the primary function of "modeling" in behavior analysis?

- A. To provide reinforcement for appropriate behavior

- B. To provide punishment for inappropriate behavior

- C. To demonstrate a target behavior for the individual to imitate

- D. To eliminate all stimuli in the environment

- Answer: C

- Explanation: The primary function of modeling is to demonstrate a target behavior for the individual to imitate or learn from the example.

71. What does it mean when a behavior analyst uses the term "tact" in the context of verbal behavior analysis?

- A. A request for reinforcement

- B. A label for a nonverbal stimulus in the environment

- C. A verbal behavior targeted for reduction

- D. A form of punishment

- Answer: B

- Explanation: In verbal behavior analysis, a "tact" is a verbal response that serves as a label for a nonverbal stimulus in the environment. It is often a description or label of something in the individual's surroundings.

72. What is a "high-probability instructional sequence" used for in behavior analysis?

- A. To teach low-probability behaviors

- B. To reinforce all behaviors equally

- C. To reduce all behaviors to low probability

- D. To promote high-probability behaviors before low-probability behaviors

- Answer: D

- Explanation: A high-probability instructional sequence is used to promote high-probability behaviors before low-probability behaviors to increase the likelihood of compliance and successful teaching.

73. What is the term for a reduction in behavior when reinforcement is provided for a behavior that is less frequent or lower in magnitude compared to the target behavior?

- A. Extinction

- B. Shaping

- C. Reinforcement

- D. Response cost

- Answer: D

- Explanation: Response cost is a procedure that involves a reduction in behavior when reinforcement is provided for a behavior that is less frequent or lower in magnitude compared to the target behavior.

74. In behavior analysis, what is the term for the process of reinforcing successive approximations of a target behavior?

- A. Reinforcement burst

- B. Shaping

- C. Generalization

- D. Extinction burst

- Answer: B

- Explanation: Shaping is the process of reinforcing successive approximations of a target behavior, which involves reinforcing behaviors that are similar but not identical to the desired behavior.

75. What is a "chained schedule" in behavior analysis?

- A. A schedule for reinforcement

- B. A sequence of discrete behaviors linked together

- C. A reinforcement procedure using tokens

- D. A form of punishment

- Answer: B

- Explanation: A chained schedule involves a sequence of discrete behaviors linked together, with each behavior serving as a cue for the next behavior in the chain.

76. In behavior analysis, what is a "behavior contract" used for?

- A. To diagnose psychological disorders

- B. To establish a controlled environment with no external stimuli

- C. To reinforce appropriate behavior using tokens or points

- D. To specify the conditions under which reinforcement will be delivered based on the client's behavior

- Answer: D

- Explanation: A behavior contract is used to specify the conditions under which reinforcement will be delivered based on the client's behavior. It often outlines the expectations and consequences.

77. What is "response maintenance" in behavior analysis?

- A. The act of repeating a behavior consistently

- B. The process of extending the effects of an intervention over time

- C. The strengthening of a behavior by removing an aversive stimulus

- D. The process of extinguishing a behavior

- Answer: B

- Explanation: Response maintenance refers to the process of extending the effects of an intervention over time, ensuring that the behavior continues in the absence of ongoing intervention.

78. In behavior analysis, what does the term "covert behavior" refer to?

- A. Behavior that is observable and can be directly measured

- B. Behavior that is not influenced by reinforcement or punishment

- C. Behavior that occurs in private, inside an individual's mind

- D. Behavior that is rarely seen in clinical settings

- Answer: C

- Explanation: Covert behavior refers to behavior that occurs in private, inside an individual's mind, and is not directly observable.

79. What is a "multiple baseline design" used for in single-subject research?

- A. A design with multiple treatment phases

- B. A design in which multiple behaviors are assessed within the same subject

- C. A design involving multiple subjects

- D. A design with multiple dependent variables

- Answer: B

- Explanation: In single-subject research, a multiple baseline design is used to assess multiple behaviors within the same subject to evaluate the effects of an intervention across behaviors.

80. In behavior analysis, what is a "stimulus preference assessment" used for?

- A. To identify the antecedents and consequences that maintain problem behaviors

- B. To determine the duration of problem behaviors

- C. To establish reinforcement schedules

- D. To identify the stimuli preferred by a client for use in behavior-change programs

- Answer: D

- Explanation: A stimulus preference assessment is used to identify the stimuli preferred by a client for use in behavior-change programs, helping to determine effective reinforcers.

81. What is a "behavior reduction plan" used for in behavior analysis?

- A. To increase the frequency of problem behaviors

- B. To reinforce all behaviors

- C. To decrease the frequency of problem behaviors

- D. To establish reinforcement schedules

- Answer: C

- Explanation: A behavior reduction plan is used to decrease the frequency of problem behaviors through the use of interventions and strategies designed to eliminate or reduce the target behaviors.

82. In behavior analysis, what is the term for a schedule of reinforcement where the number of responses required for reinforcement varies unpredictably?

- A. Fixed-Interval Schedule

- B. Variable-Interval Schedule

- C. Fixed-Ratio Schedule

- D. Variable-Ratio Schedule

- Answer: D

- Explanation: In a variable-ratio schedule, the number of responses required for reinforcement varies unpredictably.

83. What is "prompt delay" in behavior analysis?

- A. A procedure for presenting a prompt before the target behavior

- B. A procedure for delaying reinforcement to assess extinction

- C. A procedure for gradually increasing the intensity of prompts

- D. A procedure for presenting a prompt after a delay to teach a behavior

- Answer: D

- Explanation: Prompt delay is a procedure in which a prompt is presented after a delay following the target behavior to teach a behavior.

84. In behavior analysis, what is the term for a stimulus that initially has no effect on a behavior but becomes a conditioned reinforcer through pairing with other reinforcers?

- A. Conditioned stimulus

- B. Neutral stimulus

- C. Unconditioned stimulus

- D. Discriminative stimulus

- Answer: B

- Explanation: A neutral stimulus is a stimulus that initially has no effect on a behavior but becomes a conditioned reinforcer through pairing with other reinforcers.

85. What is the term for a schedule of reinforcement where reinforcement is provided for only some correct responses?

- A. Continuous reinforcement

- B. Variable-ratio schedule

- C. Fixed-interval schedule

- D. Variable-interval schedule

- Answer: B

- Explanation: In a variable-ratio schedule, reinforcement is provided for only some correct responses, and the number of responses required varies unpredictably.

86. What is "intermittent reinforcement" used for in behavior analysis?

- A. To consistently reinforce a behavior

- B. To reinforce a behavior at the same rate

- C. To provide reinforcement for every occurrence of a behavior

- D. To reinforce a behavior occasionally or sporadically

- Answer: D

- Explanation: Intermittent reinforcement is used to reinforce a behavior occasionally or sporadically, not every time the behavior occurs.

87. In behavior analysis, what is the term for a stimulus that serves as a cue for a specific behavior and signals that reinforcement is available for that behavior under certain conditions?

- A. Neutral stimulus

- B. Unconditioned stimulus

- C. Discriminative stimulus

- D. Conditioned stimulus

- Answer: C

- Explanation: A discriminative stimulus (SD) serves as a cue for a specific behavior and signals that reinforcement is available for that behavior under certain conditions.

88. What is a "differential reinforcement" used for in behavior analysis?

- A. To consistently reinforce all behaviors

- B. To reinforce the occurrence of problem behaviors

- C. To reinforce a target behavior while not reinforcing other behaviors

- D. To provide reinforcement for all behaviors equally

- Answer: C

- Explanation: Differential reinforcement is used to reinforce a target behavior while not reinforcing other behaviors, thus reducing or eliminating those other behaviors.

89. In behavior analysis, what is a "response burst"?

- A. A sudden decrease in the frequency of a behavior

- B. A temporary increase in the frequency and intensity of a behavior when reinforcement is provided

- C. A gradual decrease in behavior over time

- D. A pattern of responding that is consistent and predictable

- Answer: B

- Explanation: A response burst is a temporary increase in the frequency and intensity of a behavior when reinforcement is provided.

90. What is the term for a schedule of reinforcement where reinforcement is provided for the first correct response after a fixed amount of time has passed?

- A. Fixed-Ratio Schedule

- B. Variable-Ratio Schedule

- C. Fixed-Interval Schedule

- D. Variable-Interval Schedule

- Answer: C

- Explanation: In a fixed-interval schedule, reinforcement is provided for the first correct response after a fixed amount of time has passed.

91. What is "response cost" used for in behavior analysis?

- A. To increase the frequency of problem behaviors

- B. To eliminate the effects of reinforcement

- C. To reduce the frequency or magnitude of a problem behavior by removing a specified amount of reinforcement

- D. To increase the strength of a behavior by adding reinforcement

- Answer: C

- Explanation: Response cost is used to reduce the frequency or magnitude of a problem behavior by removing a specified amount of reinforcement contingent on the occurrence of the behavior.

92. In behavior analysis, what does the term "contingency" refer to?

- A. A sequence of behaviors linked together

- B. A sequence of environmental stimuli

- C. A specific relationship between a behavior and its consequences

- D. A type of punishment

- Answer: C

- Explanation: A contingency in behavior analysis refers to a specific relationship between a behavior and its consequences, which can be reinforcement or punishment.

93. What is the term for a reduction in behavior when reinforcement is no longer provided for that behavior?

- A. Shaping

- B. Reinforcement

- C. Extinction

- D. Response cost

- Answer: C

- Explanation: Extinction refers to a reduction in behavior when reinforcement is no longer provided for that behavior.

94. What is "functional communication training" used for in behavior analysis?

- A. To eliminate all communication

- B. To teach non-functional communication skills

- C. To replace problem behaviors with appropriate communication skills

- D. To reinforce inappropriate communication

- Answer: C

- Explanation: Functional communication training is used to replace problem behaviors with appropriate communication skills, allowing individuals to express their needs and wants effectively.

95. In behavior analysis, what is "task analysis" used for?

- A. To analyze the effectiveness of reinforcement

- B. To analyze the environmental stimuli

- C. To break down complex behaviors into smaller, teachable components

- D. To analyze covert behaviors

- Answer: C

- Explanation: Task analysis is used to break down complex behaviors into smaller, teachable components, making it easier to teach and assess the individual's skills.

96. What does the term "mand" refer to in the context of verbal behavior analysis?

- A. A form of covert behavior

- B. A request for reinforcement or assistance

- C. A label for a nonverbal stimulus

- D. A form of punishment

- Answer: B

- Explanation: In verbal behavior analysis, a "mand" is a verbal request for reinforcement or assistance, such as asking for food, attention, or help.

97. What is "stimulus control transfer" used for in behavior analysis?

- A. To transfer a response from one individual to another

- B. To shift control of behavior from one stimulus to another

- C. To transfer behavior from one setting to another

- D. To shift control of behavior from the environment to the individual

- Answer: B

- Explanation: Stimulus control transfer is used to shift control of behavior from one stimulus to another, often from a prompt or cue to a natural or less intrusive cue.

98. In behavior analysis, what is the term for "observational learning" or learning through observing others' behavior and its consequences?

- A. Operant conditioning

- B. Classical conditioning

- C. Social learning

- D. Differential reinforcement

- Answer: C

- Explanation: Observational learning or learning through observing others' behavior and its consequences is often referred to as social learning.

99. What is a "generalization gradient" used for in behavior analysis?

- A. A measurement of the intensity of reinforcement

- B. A graph showing the decline in behavior over time

- C. A graph showing the spread of a behavior across different situations or stimuli

- D. A measurement of response latency

- Answer: C

- Explanation: A generalization gradient is a graph showing the spread or extent to which a behavior occurs across different situations or stimuli.

100. What is "response latency" in behavior analysis?

- A. The time it takes for a response to occur after a stimulus is presented

- B. The number of responses within a certain time frame

- C. The duration of a response

- D. The intensity of a response

- Answer: A

- Explanation: Response latency is the time it takes for a response to occur after a stimulus is presented.

Section 1: Foundations of Applied Behavior Analysis

What are the core dimensions of applied behavior analysis as defined by Baer, Wolf, & Risley (1968)?

A. Behavior, reinforcement, punishment, stimulus control

B. Behavior, measurement, analysis, verification

C. Behavior, environment, function, treatment

D. Behavior, analytic, socially significant, effective

Answer: D

Explanation: The core dimensions of applied behavior analysis (ABA) defined by Baer, Wolf, & Risley are often remembered as the BE-SAFE acronym: Behavior, Analytic, Socially significant, Effective.

What is the key assumption of radical behaviorism?

A. Behavior is solely influenced by genetics

B. Behavior is primarily shaped by cognitive processes

C. Behavior is determined by the individual's internal state

D. Behavior is governed by environmental factors and learning history

Answer: D

Explanation: Radical behaviorism asserts that behavior is governed by environmental factors and learning history, emphasizing the influence of the external environment.

What is the primary focus of the experimental analysis of behavior?

A. Assessing and diagnosing psychological disorders

B. Understanding the cognitive processes underlying behavior

C. Evaluating the effects of environmental variables on behavior

D. Examining the biological basis of behavior

Answer: C

Explanation: The primary focus of the experimental analysis of behavior is to evaluate the effects of environmental variables on behavior through controlled experiments.

What distinguishes applied behavior analysis (ABA) from other fields related to behavior?

A. The use of cognitive interventions

B. The focus on neurological aspects of behavior

C. The emphasis on real-world application and social significance

D. The exclusion of behavior modification

Answer: C

Explanation: ABA is distinct from other fields by its emphasis on real-world application and socially significant behavior change.

How would you define "contingency" in the context of applied behavior analysis (ABA)?

A. A cause-and-effect relationship between variables

B. A description of covert behavior

C. A synonym for reinforcement

D. A condition under which punishment is administered

Answer: A

Explanation: In ABA, a contingency refers to a cause-and-effect relationship between variables, where one event depends on the occurrence of another.

What is the term for behavior that is shaped and maintained by verbal instructions or rules?

A. Operant behavior

B. Respondent behavior

C. Rule-governed behavior

D. Automatic behavior

Answer: C

Explanation: Rule-governed behavior is behavior that is shaped and maintained by verbal instructions or rules.

How would you classify the use of a stopwatch to measure the duration of a behavior?

A. A direct measure

B. An indirect measure

C. A continuous measure

D. A rate measure

Answer: A

Explanation: Using a stopwatch to measure the duration of a behavior is considered a direct measure because it directly assesses the behavior of interest.

What is the primary purpose of graphing data in behavior analysis?

A. To make the data look visually appealing

B. To highlight individual variations in behavior

C. To communicate and analyze quantitative relations between variables

D. To demonstrate the complexity of behavior

Answer: C

Explanation: The primary purpose of graphing data in behavior analysis is to communicate and analyze quantitative relations between variables, making it easier to understand behavior patterns.

Which of the following is NOT one of the four dimensions of behavior that should be measured?

A. Intensity

B. Latency

C. Inter-Response Time

D. Quality

Answer: C

Explanation: Intensity, latency, and quality are dimensions of behavior that should be measured. Inter-Response Time is not typically a dimension of behavior.

What is the term for a schedule of reinforcement where reinforcement is provided for every occurrence of a behavior?

A. Fixed-Ratio Schedule

B. Continuous Reinforcement Schedule

C. Variable-Ratio Schedule

D. Variable-Interval Schedule

Answer: B

Explanation: In a continuous reinforcement schedule, reinforcement is provided for every occurrence of a behavior.

Section 2: Concepts and Principles

What is the term for a stimulus that naturally and automatically elicits a response without prior learning or conditioning?

A. Conditioned stimulus

B. Neutral stimulus

C. Unconditioned stimulus

D. Discriminative stimulus

Answer: C

Explanation: An unconditioned stimulus is a stimulus that naturally and automatically elicits a response without prior learning or conditioning.

In behavior analysis, what is a "behavioral contingency"?

A. A contract outlining behavioral expectations

B. The relationship between a behavior and its consequences

C. A type of punishment procedure

D. A reinforcement schedule

Answer: B

Explanation: A behavioral contingency refers to the relationship between a behavior and its consequences, defining how behavior is influenced by its outcomes.

What is the term for reinforcing a behavior by adding something desirable to the environment?

A. Positive reinforcement

B. Negative reinforcement

C. Positive punishment

D. Negative punishment

Answer: A

Explanation: Positive reinforcement involves reinforcing a behavior by adding something desirable to the environment, which increases the likelihood of the behavior occurring again.

In behavior analysis, what is the term for a behavior that is more likely to occur in the future as a result of the presentation or addition of a stimulus?

A. Respondent behavior

B. Operant behavior

C. Discriminative stimulus

D. Discriminative response

Answer: B

Explanation: Operant behavior is a behavior that is more likely to occur in the future as a result of the presentation or addition of a stimulus.

What is the term for a schedule of reinforcement where reinforcement is provided for the first correct response after a fixed number of responses?

A. Fixed-Ratio Schedule

B. Variable-Ratio Schedule

C. Fixed-Interval Schedule

D. Variable-Interval Schedule

Answer: A

Explanation: In a fixed-ratio schedule, reinforcement is provided for the first correct response after a fixed number of responses.

What is the term for reinforcing a behavior by removing or avoiding something aversive from the environment?

A. Positive reinforcement

B. Negative reinforcement

C. Positive punishment

D. Negative punishment

Answer: B

Explanation: Negative reinforcement involves reinforcing a behavior by removing or avoiding something aversive from the environment, which increases the likelihood of the behavior occurring again.

What is "response cost" used for in behavior analysis?

A. To increase the frequency of problem behaviors

B. To eliminate the effects of reinforcement

C. To reduce the frequency or magnitude of a problem behavior by removing a specified amount of reinforcement

D. To increase the strength of a behavior by adding reinforcement

Answer: C

Explanation: Response cost is used to reduce the frequency or magnitude of a problem behavior by removing a specified amount of reinforcement contingent on the occurrence of the behavior.

What is "response latency" in behavior analysis?

A. The time it takes for a response to occur after a stimulus is presented

B. The number of responses within a certain time frame

C. The duration of a response

D. The intensity of a response

Answer: A

Explanation: Response latency is the time it takes for a response to occur after a stimulus is presented.

What is the term for a reduction in behavior when reinforcement is no longer provided for that behavior?

A. Shaping

B. Reinforcement

C. Extinction

D. Response cost

Answer: C

Explanation: Extinction refers to a reduction in behavior when reinforcement is no longer provided for that behavior.

What is the term for a schedule of reinforcement where reinforcement is provided for the first correct response after a variable amount of time has passed?

A. Fixed-Ratio Schedule

B. Variable-Ratio Schedule

C. Fixed-Interval Schedule

D. Variable-Interval Schedule

Answer: D

Explanation: In a variable-interval schedule, reinforcement is provided for the first correct response after a variable amount of time has passed.

Section 3: Ethics

What is the primary responsibility of a behavior analyst in the context of ethics?

A. Ensuring the comfort of the client during assessments

B. Conducting research to advance the field

C. Promoting client welfare and well-being

D. Upholding the code of silence regarding ethical issues

Answer: C

Explanation: The primary responsibility of a behavior analyst in the context of ethics is promoting client welfare and well-being.

According to the Professional and Ethical Compliance Code for Behavior Analysts, what is a behavior analyst's responsibility to clients?

A. To prioritize financial gain for the behavior analyst

B. To provide the least restrictive environment for the client

C. To ensure that services are evidence-based

D. To protect the confidentiality of the client

Answer: D

Explanation: According to the Professional and Ethical Compliance Code for Behavior Analysts, a behavior analyst's responsibility to clients includes protecting the confidentiality of the client.

In the context of ethics, what is the term for maintaining high standards of competence in the field?

A. Professional responsibility

B. Continuing education

C. Supervision

D. Maintenance of professional relationships

Answer: B

Explanation: Maintaining high standards of competence in the field is often achieved through continuing education, which is an ethical responsibility.

What is the role of the Responsible Conduct of Behavior Analysts section in the Professional and Ethical Compliance Code for Behavior Analysts?

A. To outline ethical considerations for research studies

B. To define the boundaries of confidentiality

C. To provide guidance on ethical issues in supervision and management

D. To establish rules for client billing

Answer: C

Explanation: The Responsible Conduct of Behavior Analysts section in the code provides guidance on ethical issues in supervision and management.

In the context of ethics, what does the term "conflict of interest" refer to?

A. A situation where the client is not interested in receiving services

B. A situation where a behavior analyst has a personal interest that may compromise their professional judgment

C. A disagreement between colleagues in the field

D. A dispute over billing procedures

Answer: B

Explanation: A conflict of interest refers to a situation where a behavior analyst has a personal interest that may compromise their professional judgment, potentially leading to bias.

Section 4: Behavior Assessment

What is the purpose of conducting a functional assessment of problem behavior?

A. To diagnose psychological disorders

B. To identify the stimuli preferred by the client

C. To determine the duration of problem behaviors

D. To identify the environmental variables influencing the problem behavior

Answer: D

Explanation: The purpose of conducting a functional assessment of problem behavior is to identify the environmental variables (antecedents and consequences) influencing the problem behavior.

In the context of behavior assessment, what is the primary goal of conducting a preference assessment?

A. To determine the client's preferred schedule of reinforcement

B. To identify the client's favorite activities and items for use in reinforcement

C. To identify the stimuli that evoke problem behaviors

D. To measure the intensity of problem behaviors

Answer: B

Explanation: The primary goal of conducting a preference assessment is to identify the client's favorite activities and items that can be used as reinforcement.

What is the term for a procedure that involves systematically observing and recording behavior in its natural environment?

A. Functional analysis

B. Experimental analysis

C. Descriptive assessment

D. Discrete trial training

Answer: C

Explanation: A descriptive assessment involves systematically observing and recording behavior in its natural environment without manipulating variables.

What is the primary goal of a functional analysis of problem behavior?

A. To determine the intensity of problem behaviors

B. To diagnose psychological disorders

C. To identify the environmental variables influencing problem behavior

D. To assess the client's preferences for reinforcement

Answer: C

Explanation: The primary goal of a functional analysis of problem behavior is to identify the environmental variables (antecedents and consequences) influencing the problem behavior.

In behavior assessment, what is the term for a procedure that involves the manipulation of antecedent and consequent variables to determine their effects on behavior?

A. Descriptive assessment

B. Experimental analysis

C. Functional analysis

D. Functional communication training

Answer: B

Explanation: Experimental analysis involves the manipulation of antecedent and consequent variables to determine their effects on behavior in a controlled setting.

Section 5: Behavior-Change Procedures

What is the primary goal of positive reinforcement procedures in behavior change?

A. To increase the frequency of problem behaviors

B. To eliminate problem behaviors completely

C. To strengthen and increase the frequency of appropriate behaviors

D. To eliminate all behaviors except a single target behavior

Answer: C

Explanation: The primary goal of positive reinforcement procedures is to strengthen and increase the frequency of appropriate behaviors.

What is the term for an intervention that is based on the concept of "stimulus control"?

A. Extinction

B. Shaping

C. Chaining

D. Prompting

Answer: D

Explanation: Prompting is an intervention based on the concept of "stimulus control," where additional cues or prompts are provided to guide behavior.

What is the primary purpose of using extinction as a behavior-change procedure?

A. To increase the occurrence of a behavior

B. To strengthen the behavior by adding reinforcement

C. To eliminate the behavior by removing reinforcement

D. To increase the intensity of a behavior

Answer: C

Explanation: The primary purpose of using extinction is to eliminate a behavior by removing reinforcement.

In behavior analysis, what is the term for a procedure that involves reducing problem behavior by reinforcing an alternative behavior that serves the same function?

A. Differential reinforcement of other behavior (DRO)

B. Differential reinforcement of low rates of responding (DRL)

C. Differential reinforcement of alternative behavior (DRA)

D. Differential reinforcement of incompatible behavior (DRI)

Answer: C

Explanation: Differential reinforcement of alternative behavior (DRA) involves reducing problem behavior by reinforcing an alternative behavior that serves the same function.

What is "stimulus fading" used for in behavior analysis?

A. To increase the intensity of a behavior

B. To reduce the frequency of problem behaviors

C. To shift control of a behavior from one stimulus to another

D. To increase the strength of a behavior by adding reinforcement

Answer: C

Explanation: Stimulus fading is used to shift control of a behavior from one stimulus to another, often from a prompt to a natural cue.

What is the term for a behavior-change procedure that involves reinforcing successive approximations to a target behavior?

A. Shaping

B. Chaining

C. Extinction

D. Prompting

Answer: A

Explanation: Shaping is a behavior-change procedure that involves reinforcing successive approximations to a target behavior until the full target behavior is achieved.

What is "chaining" used for in behavior analysis?

A. To increase the intensity of a behavior

B. To reduce the frequency of problem behaviors

C. To teach a sequence of behaviors as a single complex behavior

D. To increase the strength of a behavior by adding reinforcement

Answer: C

Explanation: Chaining is used to teach a sequence of behaviors as a single complex behavior by breaking it down into smaller, teachable steps.

What is "discrete-trial teaching" used for in behavior analysis?

A. To reinforce problem behaviors

B. To teach complex behavior chains

C. To conduct functional assessments

D. To teach simple skills in a structured and controlled manner

Answer: D

Explanation: Discrete-trial teaching is used to teach simple skills in a structured and controlled manner, often used with individuals with developmental disorders.

What is the primary goal of teaching "discriminative stimuli" in behavior analysis?

A. To increase the frequency of problem behaviors

B. To strengthen operant behavior

C. To increase the intensity of a behavior

D. To establish the conditions under which a behavior will be reinforced

Answer: D

Explanation: The primary goal of teaching discriminative stimuli is to establish the conditions under which a behavior will be reinforced.

What is the term for a procedure used to promote the generalization of a behavior across different settings or stimuli?

A. Response cost

B. Shaping

C. Fading

D. Generalization training

Answer: D

Explanation: Generalization training involves procedures to promote the generalization of a behavior across different settings or stimuli.

Section 6: Personnel Supervision And Management

What is the primary reason for using behavior-analytic supervision in the field of applied behavior analysis?

A. To create a hierarchical structure within organizations

B. To advance the career of supervisees

C. To ensure compliance with regulatory agencies

D. To improve the quality of behavior-analytic services

Answer: D

Explanation: The primary reason for using behavior-analytic supervision is to improve the quality of behavior-analytic services, which includes ensuring that clients receive the most effective and ethical treatment.

What should be the main focus when selecting supervision goals for a supervisee?

A. Advancing the supervisee's career

B. Achieving the most efficient service delivery

C. Addressing the supervisee's personal goals

D. Meeting the needs of clients

Answer: D

Explanation: The main focus when selecting supervision goals for a supervisee should be meeting the needs of clients, as the ultimate goal is to provide effective and ethical services.

In behavior-analytic supervision, what does "performance monitoring" entail?

A. Monitoring the financial performance of the organization

B. Monitoring the behavior of clients

C. Monitoring the performance of the supervisor

D. Monitoring the supervisee's performance and providing feedback

Answer: D

Explanation: Performance monitoring in behavior-analytic supervision involves monitoring the supervisee's performance and providing feedback to help them improve their skills.

What is a "functional assessment approach" in the context of personnel supervision and management?

A. Evaluating the supervisor's performance

B. Assessing the client's progress

C. Using a behavior-analytic approach to identify variables affecting personnel performance

D. Conducting a functional analysis of problem behavior

Answer: C

Explanation: A functional assessment approach in personnel supervision and management involves using a behavior-analytic approach to identify variables affecting personnel performance.

What is the primary purpose of using function-based strategies to improve personnel performance in behavior-analytic supervision?

A. To establish strict control over supervisees

B. To eliminate client rights

C. To ensure compliance with organizational rules

D. To improve client outcomes and the effectiveness of services

Answer: D

Explanation: The primary purpose of using function-based strategies to improve personnel performance in behavior-analytic supervision is to improve client outcomes and the effectiveness of services provided.

Section 7: BCBA Exam Practice Questions with Answers and Explanations

When a behavior analyst conducts multiple tests of her therapy before writing it in a formal behavior program, she is sticking to which basic assumption of behavior analysis?

A. Determination

B. The Parsimony Law

C. Empiricism

D. None of the preceding

Answer: C

Explanation: The behavior analyst is adhering to the basic assumption of empiricism by relying on evidence and data to guide her decisions and treatment plans.

In applied behavior analysis (ABA), what is the term for a systematic approach to solving behavior problems that involves applying principles of behavior?

A. Functional behavior assessment

B. Behavior intervention plan

C. Applied behavior analysis

D. Clinical judgment

Answer: C

Explanation: Applied behavior analysis (ABA) is a systematic approach to solving behavior problems by applying principles of behavior to design effective interventions.

What is the primary goal of a behavior intervention plan (BIP) in applied behavior analysis (ABA)?

A. To diagnose psychological disorders

B. To assess the client's preferences

C. To provide a structured schedule of reinforcement

D. To decrease problem behaviors and increase appropriate behaviors

Answer: D

Explanation: The primary goal of a behavior intervention plan (BIP) is to decrease problem behaviors and increase appropriate behaviors.

In the context of applied behavior analysis, what does the term "antecedent" refer to?

A. A consequence following a behavior

B. A behavior that is shaped by reinforcement

C. A condition or event that precedes a behavior

D. A procedure to eliminate problem behaviors

Answer: C

Explanation: In applied behavior analysis, the term "antecedent" refers to a condition or event that precedes a behavior and may influence its occurrence.

What is the term for a procedure in applied behavior analysis (ABA) that involves reducing problem behavior by systematically increasing the response effort required to engage in the behavior?

A. Positive punishment

B. Negative reinforcement

C. Response cost

D. Differential reinforcement

Answer: C

Explanation: Response cost is a procedure in applied behavior analysis that involves reducing problem behavior by systematically increasing the response effort required to engage in the behavior.

Section 8: BCBA Exam Practice Questions (Cont.)

In applied behavior analysis (ABA), what does the term "target behavior" refer to?

A. The behavior the analyst wishes to exhibit

B. The client's least favorite behavior

C. The behavior selected for change or intervention

D. The behavior that is least likely to change

Answer: C

Explanation: In ABA, the term "target behavior" refers to the behavior that is selected for change or intervention.

What is the term for a procedure that involves presenting a stimulus contingent on a behavior, leading to an increase in the future occurrence of that behavior?

A. Positive reinforcement

B. Negative reinforcement

C. Positive punishment

D. Negative punishment

Answer: A

Explanation: Positive reinforcement involves presenting a stimulus contingent on a behavior, leading to an increase in the future occurrence of that behavior.

In applied behavior analysis (ABA), what does the term "baseline" refer to?

A. The average level of a behavior before any intervention is applied

B. The most intense level of a behavior

C. The highest level of a behavior observed during a behavior intervention

D. The level of a behavior after reinforcement has been discontinued

Answer: A

Explanation: In ABA, "baseline" refers to the average level of a behavior before any intervention is applied, serving as a point of comparison.

What is the term for a procedure that involves presenting a stimulus contingent on a behavior, leading to a decrease in the future occurrence of that behavior?

A. Positive reinforcement

B. Negative reinforcement

C. Positive punishment

D. Negative punishment

Answer: C

Explanation: Positive punishment involves presenting a stimulus contingent on a behavior, leading to a decrease in the future occurrence of that behavior.

In applied behavior analysis (ABA), what does the term "functional analysis" refer to?

A. A detailed description of the client's behavior

B. A systematic evaluation of the client's preferences

C. A procedure to identify the environmental variables influencing problem behavior

D. A clinical assessment of the client's mental health

Answer: C

Explanation: In ABA, "functional analysis" refers to a procedure to identify the environmental variables (antecedents and consequences) influencing problem behavior.

Section 9: BCBA Exam Practice Questions (Cont.)

In applied behavior analysis (ABA), what is the term for a procedure that involves reinforcing a behavior by removing or avoiding something aversive from the environment to?

A. Positive reinforcement

B. Negative reinforcement

C. Positive punishment

D. Negative punishment

Answer: B

Explanation: Negative reinforcement involves reinforcing a behavior by removing or avoiding something aversive from the environment, which increases the likelihood of the behavior occurring again.

What is "response cost" used for in behavior analysis?

A. To increase the frequency of problem behaviors

B. To eliminate the effects of reinforcement

C. To reduce the frequency or magnitude of a problem behavior by removing a specified amount of reinforcement

D. To increase the strength of a behavior by adding reinforcement

Answer: C

Explanation: Response cost is used to reduce the frequency or magnitude of a problem behavior by removing a specified amount of reinforcement contingent on the occurrence of the behavior.

What is "response latency" in behavior analysis?

A. The time it takes for a response to occur after a stimulus is presented

B. The number of responses within a certain time frame

C. The duration of a response

D. The intensity of a response

Answer: A

Explanation: Response latency is the time it takes for a response to occur after a stimulus is presented.

What is the term for a reduction in behavior when reinforcement is no longer provided for that behavior?

A. Shaping

B. Reinforcement

C. Extinction

D. Response cost

Answer: C

Explanation: Extinction refers to a reduction in behavior when reinforcement is no longer provided for that behavior.

What is the term for a schedule of reinforcement where reinforcement is provided for the first correct response after a variable amount of time has passed?

A. Fixed-Ratio Schedule

B. Variable-Ratio Schedule

C. Fixed-Interval Schedule

D. Variable-Interval Schedule

Answer: D

Explanation: In a variable-interval schedule, reinforcement is provided for the first correct response after a variable amount of time has passed.

What is the term for a procedure that involves systematically observing and recording behavior in its natural environment?

A. Functional analysis

B. Experimental analysis

C. Descriptive assessment

D. Discrete trial training

Answer: C

Explanation: A descriptive assessment involves systematically observing and recording behavior in its natural environment without manipulating variables.

What is the primary goal of a functional analysis of problem behavior?

A. To determine the intensity of problem behaviors

B. To diagnose psychological disorders

C. To identify the environmental variables influencing problem behavior

D. To assess the client's preferences for reinforcement

Answer: C

Explanation: The primary goal of a functional analysis of problem behavior is to identify the environmental variables (antecedents and consequences) influencing the problem behavior.

In behavior assessment, what is the term for a procedure that involves the manipulation of antecedent and consequent variables to determine their effects on behavior?

A. Descriptive assessment

B. Experimental analysis

C. Functional analysis

D. Functional communication training

Answer: B

Explanation: Experimental analysis involves the manipulation of antecedent and consequent variables to determine their effects on behavior in a controlled setting.

In the context of behavior assessment, what is the primary goal of conducting a preference assessment?

A. To determine the client's preferred schedule of reinforcement

B. To identify the client's favorite activities and items for use in reinforcement

C. To identify the stimuli that evoke problem behaviors

D. To measure the intensity of problem behaviors

Answer: B

Explanation: The primary goal of conducting a preference assessment is to identify the client's favorite activities and items that can be used as reinforcement.

What is the term for a behavior-change procedure that involves reinforcing successive approximations to a target behavior?

A. Shaping

B. Chaining

C. Extinction

D. Prompting

Answer: A

Explanation: Shaping is a behavior-change procedure that involves reinforcing successive approximations to a target behavior until the full target behavior is achieved.

What is the primary goal of positive reinforcement procedures in behavior change?

A. To increase the frequency of problem behaviors

B. To eliminate problem behaviors completely

C. To strengthen and increase the frequency of appropriate behaviors

D. To eliminate all behaviors except a single target behavior

Answer: C

Explanation: The primary goal of positive reinforcement procedures is to strengthen and increase the frequency of appropriate behaviors.

What is the term for an intervention that is based on the concept of "stimulus control"?

A. Extinction

B. Shaping

C. Chaining

D. Prompting

Answer: D

Explanation: Prompting is an intervention based on the concept of "stimulus control," where additional cues or prompts are provided to guide behavior.

What is the primary purpose of using extinction as a behavior-change procedure?

A. To increase the occurrence of a behavior

B. To strengthen the behavior by adding reinforcement

C. To eliminate the behavior by removing reinforcement

D. To increase the intensity of a behavior

Answer: C

Explanation: The primary purpose of using extinction is to eliminate a behavior by removing reinforcement.

In behavior analysis, what is the term for a procedure that involves reducing problem behavior by reinforcing an alternative behavior that serves the same function?

A. Differential reinforcement of other behavior (DRO)

B. Differential reinforcement of low rates of responding (DRL)

C. Differential reinforcement of alternative behavior (DRA)

D. Differential reinforcement of incompatible behavior (DRI)

Answer: C

Explanation: Differential reinforcement of alternative behavior (DRA) involves reducing problem behavior by reinforcing an alternative behavior that serves the same function.

What is "stimulus fading" used for in behavior analysis?

A. To increase the intensity of a behavior

B. To reduce the frequency of problem behaviors

C. To shift control of a behavior from one stimulus to another

D. To increase the strength of a behavior by adding reinforcement

Answer: C

Explanation: Stimulus fading is used to shift control of a behavior from one stimulus to another, often from a prompt to a natural cue.

Section 12: BCBA Exam Practice Questions (Cont.)

What is the term for a procedure used to promote the generalization of a behavior across different settings or stimuli?

A. Response cost

B. Shaping

C. Fading

D. Generalization training

Answer: D

Explanation: Generalization training involves procedures to promote the generalization of a behavior across different settings or stimuli.

In behavior-analytic supervision, what is the primary reason for using a functional assessment approach (e.g., performance diagnostics) to identify variables affecting personnel performance?

A. To place blame on supervisees for their performance

B. To meet regulatory requirements

C. To improve the quality of supervision

D. To understand the variables influencing supervisees' behavior

Answer: D

Explanation: Using a functional assessment approach in supervision helps to understand the variables influencing supervisees' behavior and provides a basis for improving their performance.

What is the term for a procedure that involves reinforcing problem behavior by providing access to a preferred item or activity contingent on the occurrence of the behavior?

A. Differential reinforcement of other behavior (DRO)

B. Differential reinforcement of high rates of responding (DRH)

C. Differential reinforcement of alternative behavior (DRA)

D. Differential reinforcement of problem behavior (DRPB)

Answer: D

Explanation: Differential reinforcement of problem behavior (DRPB) involves reinforcing problem behavior by providing access to a preferred item or activity contingent on the occurrence of the behavior.

In behavior analysis, what does "functional communication training" entail?

A. Training individuals to communicate using nonverbal gestures

B. Teaching individuals to use a variety of communication modalities

C. Training individuals to communicate effectively to access reinforcement and express needs

D. Teaching individuals to express themselves creatively through art and music

Answer: C

Explanation: Functional communication training involves training individuals to communicate effectively to access reinforcement and express their needs appropriately.

In personnel supervision and management, what is the primary goal of using function-based strategies to improve personnel performance?

A. To establish strict control over supervisees

B. To eliminate client rights

C. To ensure compliance with organizational rules

D. To improve client outcomes and the effectiveness of services

Answer: D

Explanation: The primary goal of using function-based strategies in personnel supervision is to improve client outcomes and the effectiveness of services provided.

What is the term for a procedure used to strengthen behavior by removing or avoiding an aversive stimulus contingent on the occurrence of the behavior?

A. Positive reinforcement

B. Negative reinforcement

C. Positive punishment

D. Negative punishment

Answer: B

Explanation: Negative reinforcement involves strengthening behavior by removing or avoiding an aversive stimulus contingent on the occurrence of the behavior.

In behavior analysis, what does the term "operant behavior" refer to?

A. Involuntary reflexes and physiological responses

B. Behavior that is primarily controlled by antecedent stimuli

C. Voluntary behavior that operates on the environment to produce consequences

D. Behavior that is influenced by respondent conditioning

Answer: C

Explanation: Operant behavior refers to voluntary behavior that operates on the environment to produce consequences.

What is the term for a reinforcement schedule where reinforcement is provided for every occurrence of a behavior?

A. Fixed-Ratio Schedule

B. Variable-Ratio Schedule

C. Fixed-Interval Schedule

D. Continuous Reinforcement

Answer: D

Explanation: Continuous reinforcement involves providing reinforcement for every occurrence of a behavior.

In behavior analysis, what is the term for a procedure used to eliminate a behavior by withholding reinforcement for that behavior?

A. Extinction

B. Reinforcement

C. Shaping

D. Prompting

Answer: A

Explanation: Extinction is a procedure used to eliminate a behavior by withholding reinforcement for that behavior.

What is "response cost" used for in behavior analysis?

A. To increase the frequency of problem behaviors

B. To eliminate the effects of reinforcement

C. To reduce the frequency or magnitude of a problem behavior by removing a specified amount of reinforcement

D. To increase the strength of a behavior by adding reinforcement

Answer: C

Explanation: Response cost is used to reduce the frequency or magnitude of a problem behavior by removing a specified amount of reinforcement contingent on the occurrence of the behavior.

In applied behavior analysis (ABA), what does the term "target behavior" refer to?

A. The behavior the analyst wishes to exhibit

B. The client's least favorite behavior

C. The behavior selected for change or intervention

D. The behavior that is least likely to change

Answer: C

Explanation: In ABA, the term "target behavior" refers to the behavior that is selected for change or intervention.

What is the term for a procedure that involves presenting a stimulus contingent on a behavior, leading to an increase in the future occurrence of that behavior?

A. Positive reinforcement

B. Negative reinforcement

C. Positive punishment

D. Negative punishment

Answer: A

Explanation: Positive reinforcement involves presenting a stimulus contingent on a behavior, leading to an increase in the future occurrence of that behavior.

In applied behavior analysis (ABA), what does the term "baseline" refer to?

A. The average level of a behavior before any intervention is applied

B. The most intense level of a behavior

C. The highest level of a behavior observed during a behavior intervention

D. The level of a behavior after reinforcement has been discontinued

Answer: A

Explanation: In ABA, "baseline" refers to the average level of a behavior before any intervention is applied, serving as a point of comparison.

What is the term for a procedure that involves presenting a stimulus contingent on a behavior, leading to a decrease in the future occurrence of that behavior?

A. Positive reinforcement

B. Negative reinforcement

C. Positive punishment

D. Negative punishment

Answer: C

Explanation: Positive punishment involves presenting a stimulus contingent on a behavior, leading to a decrease in the future occurrence of that behavior.

In applied behavior analysis (ABA), what does the term "functional analysis" refer to?

A. A detailed description of the client's behavior

B. A systematic evaluation of the client's preferences

C. A procedure to identify the environmental variables influencing problem behavior

D. A clinical assessment of the client's mental health

Answer: C

Explanation: In ABA, "functional analysis" refers to a procedure to identify the environmental variables (antecedents and consequences) influencing problem behavior.

What is the term for a procedure used to reinforce problem behavior by providing access to a preferred item or activity contingent on the occurrence of the behavior?

A. Differential reinforcement of other behavior (DRO)

B. Differential reinforcement of high rates of responding (DRH)

C. Differential reinforcement of alternative behavior (DRA)

D. Differential reinforcement of problem behavior (DRPB)

Answer: D

Explanation: Differential reinforcement of problem behavior (DRPB) involves reinforcing problem behavior by providing access to a preferred item or activity contingent on the occurrence of the behavior.

In behavior analysis, what does the term "behavioral momentum" refer to?

A. The tendency for behavior to increase in strength or resistance to change

B. The strength of a behavior's topography

C. The influence of antecedents on behavior

D. The assessment of operant behaviors

Answer: A

Explanation: Behavioral momentum refers to the tendency for behavior to increase in strength or resistance to change, often observed when high-probability behaviors precede low-probability behaviors.

In applied behavior analysis, what does "functional communication training" involve?

A. Training individuals to use nonverbal communication methods

B. Teaching individuals to express themselves through art and music

C. Training individuals to communicate effectively to access reinforcement and express their needs

D. Using sign language as the primary means of communication

Answer: C

Explanation: Functional communication training involves training individuals to communicate effectively to access reinforcement and express their needs appropriately.

What is "response cost" used for in behavior analysis?

A. To increase the frequency of problem behaviors

B. To eliminate the effects of reinforcement

C. To reduce the frequency or magnitude of a problem behavior by removing a specified amount of reinforcement

D. To increase the strength of a behavior by adding reinforcement

Answer: C

Explanation: Response cost is used to reduce the frequency or magnitude of a problem behavior by removing a specified amount of reinforcement contingent on the occurrence of the behavior.

In behavior analysis, what does "stimulus control" refer to?

A. The process of modifying antecedents and consequences to change behavior

B. The ability of a specific stimulus to evoke or occasion a specific response

C. The use of aversive stimuli to decrease problem behavior

D. The process of shaping behavior through successive approximations

Answer: B

Explanation: Stimulus control refers to the ability of a specific stimulus to evoke or occasion a specific response.

Mr. Winston has established a reward system in his classroom, where only those kids receiving a prize from the "treasure box" are individuals who have completed homework for five out of the five days of the week.

A. co-dependent group contingency.

B. Dependent group contingency

C. independent group contingency.

D. symbiotic group contingency.

Answer(s): C

Conclusion

This comprehensive guide has provided a thorough overview of the foundational principles, concepts, and practices of applied behavior analysis (ABA), tailored to prepare aspiring behavior analysts for the Board Certified Behavior Analyst (BCBA) exam. We've explored a wide array of topics, delving into the philosophical underpinnings of behavior analysis, the core principles, measurement and data analysis, experimental design, ethics, behavior assessment, behavior-change procedures, personnel supervision, and management.

Throughout the book, we've covered the essential knowledge and skills required to excel in the field of behavior analysis and to achieve success in the BCBA exam. This journey has included an in-depth exploration of:

The goals and philosophical assumptions of behavior analysis.

Distinctions among behaviorism, the experimental analysis of behavior, applied behavior analysis, and professional practice guided by the science of behavior analysis.

The dimensions of applied behavior analysis (Baer, Wolf, & Risley, 1968).

Key concepts and principles, including reinforcement, punishment, schedules of reinforcement, extinction, stimulus control, and many more.

The importance of operational definitions and measurement procedures.

The benefits of single-subject experimental designs in comparison to group designs.

The ethical responsibilities of a behavior analyst, from their clients to supervisees and in research.

The critical steps involved in behavior assessment, including preference assessments, functional analysis, and assessment interpretation.

A wide range of behavior-change procedures, from positive reinforcement to response cost, shaping, and more.

The significance of promoting stimulus and response generalization and maintenance.

The roles and responsibilities of behavior analysts in supervision and management, with a focus on effective strategies and performance improvement.

To further enhance your learning, we provided a substantial number of practice questions along the way, offering detailed explanations to reinforce your understanding of the material. These practice questions mimic the types of questions you may encounter in the BCBA exam, enabling you to test your knowledge and readiness for the certification.

As you continue your journey to becoming a certified behavior analyst, it's important to apply the knowledge gained in this book through practical experience and real-world scenarios. The field of behavior analysis is dynamic and continually evolving, and as you progress, staying updated on the latest research and best practices is crucial.

By diligently studying and practicing the principles outlined in this guide, you'll not only be well-prepared for the BCBA exam but also equipped with the skills and expertise to make a meaningful impact on the lives of individuals with diverse needs. Behavior analysis is a field dedicated to improving the well-being and quality of life for those it serves, and your dedication to this important mission is commendable.

In the pursuit of BCBA certification, remember that success is achieved through dedication, continuous learning, and a commitment to ethical and evidence-based practices. We wish you the best of luck in your journey to becoming a Board Certified Behavior Analyst, and may you contribute to the betterment of the lives of individuals through the principles and practices of applied behavior analysis.

Thank you for reading my book all the way to the end. Now, it's high time you put what you've learned into action.

I hope you enjoyed reading it as much as I enjoyed writing it. Please leave a review of this book.